THE PROM

Other Andrew Murray titles:

The Promise of the Spirit

ANDREW MURRAY

Edited by
Simon Fox

Marshall Pickering

First published in Great Britain in 1990 by Marshall Pickering

Marshall Pickering is an imprint of
the Collins Religious Division,
part of the Collins Publishing Group,
8 Grafton Street, London W1X 3LA

ISBN 0 720 80748 4

Text set in Times by Watermark, Hampermill Cottage,
Watford WD1 4PL
Printed in Great Britain by Cox & Wyman Ltd, Reading,
Berks.

CONTENTS

Chapter 1

The Second Blessing

The Letter to the Hebrews

Both Scripture and experience teach us that in the case of a very large number of believers growth and progress in the Christian life do not happen all at once. Very many have to confess at some stage that they have left their first love for the Lord and have grown cold. Others mourn over their lack of power to conquer sin and do God's will; their most earnest prayers and efforts have failed to bring into their lives the strength and the joy they have hoped for. Throughout the Church of Christ we find many believers in a feeble, carnal and sickly spiritual state, their life and experience by no means in accord with what God has promised and is able to do. When such Christians are convicted by God's Holy Spirit of the wrongness of their condition and are led to see and accept the wonderful provision for a better life which there is in Christ, the transition is in many cases so distinct, and comes so directly from the Saviour himself, that it seems to them no less wonderful than what they received at conversion, and they feel that no better name can be found for this experience than the Second Blessing.

The question may very justly be asked, Is this according to God's Word? In order to answer that question, we shall take one of the Epistles in the New Testament and point out how the thought of there being two stages in God's dealings with his people runs through the whole of it. The Second Blessing consists in essence of this: the full and perfect knowledge of our Lord Jesus in his heavenly glory, and of the power of his Endless Life, through which all his work in us is achieved. As we look at the different illustrations of the principle of the Second Blessing which we shall find, we shall learn what are the conditions for our obtaining it.

It is the Epistle to the Hebrews that we are going to look at. There is a reason why we should find the truth we are thinking of especially illustrated here. Most of the other Epistles were written to churches composed of Gentiles or of Jews and Gentiles. This Epistle is addressed to Jews only. They had been brought up in the religion of the Old Dispensation. Although they had become Christians, they had retained much of the spirit of that Dispensation. They had not advanced as they ought to have done to the full knowledge of the complete and perfect salvation which there is in Christ. And so they have become for all time a warning to the Church against the danger of standing still and resting content with first principles. The Epistle is one of the most blessed revelations of the glory of Christ, of the perfection of his work and the completeness of the salvation which he can give us. It is a chart in which the difference between the low level of Christian life and the Better Life is clearly marked. It shows us all the paths by which we can be led away from or helped up to the life which God would have us live.

God's revelation of himself

Our first illustration of what the Second Blessing or Better Life is appears in the opening words of the Epistle: 'God, who at sundry times and in divers manners spake in time past unto the fathers by the prophets, hath in these latter days spoken to us by his Son.' Here we see the two stages in God's revelation of himself. God had (and still has) two ways of speaking to men – not one, not three, but two. The first was a preparation for the second, while the second was the fulfilment of the first. The causes of this were not arbitrary, but in the purposes of God there was a need for it. In the first stage God spoke through men – the prophets. Full, direct and immediate revelations of God were not given at that time. Only after the inadequacy of this means of revelation had been felt and a longing for a more direct divine manifestation had been awakened did the full revelation come in. Then *God spoke to us by his Son*.

This does not refer merely to the words which the Son spoke when he was on earth. If that were so, those words could very easily become mere images of divine truth, just like the words of the prophets. The words of God's Son would then occupy our minds without bringing us into direct contact with God. But God speaking through his Son means something infinitely higher than that. Jesus Christ not only has and speaks the Word of God like a prophet, but he is the Word. He is the living expression of the Father's heart, bearing in himself and imparting all the fullness of the Divine life and love. Coming out of God's heart, the Living Word enters our hearts. Out of the depths of God's heart that Word comes, and enters into the depths of our hearts. Christ dwells in our hearts as he dwells in the Father's heart. He is our life, our joy and our love, as he is the Father's. So this is what the first verse of Hebrews means when it says that God has not only spoken to us through his servants and their words, through his Book and its words, but also through his Son.

These two stages in God's revelation of himself in his dealings with his people as a whole have their counterpart in the history of the individual soul. After our conversion our religion is very much dependent upon human activities and traditions; to a large extent our faith relies upon our fellow Christians. But as the believer goes on in the spiritual life and grows weary of the failures and disappointments which he frequently meets along the way, he very often begins to long for a more definitely personal fellowship with God, for a more direct experience of his presence and power. A man begins to feel, 'In my dealings with God I have not got beyond words and thoughts and feelings. I have not yet had God speaking through his Son right into my heart.' He discovers that the Saviour has promised to come with his Father to make his abode in the believer's heart – he has promised to manifest himself in the believer's life. He begins to see how, in the Spirit of the glorified Jesus, a beautiful provision has been made for keeping up direct and unbroken communication between the Father in heaven and the child on earth. He understands how God's speaking to us through his Son opens up the possibility of a fellowship surpassing all understanding, and he can now rest content with nothing less. And as he tastes the blessedness of this direct communication of God's presence and love to the soul, he knows that 'God...who in divers manners spake in times past by the prophets' has now spoken to him, personally, by his Son.

The work of Christ

Our second illustration of the meaning of the Second Blessing is found in the work of Christ. In it, too, we find two parts. They are very clearly put before us in

Hebrews 1:3, where we read that Jesus, 'when he had by himself purged our sins, sat down on the right hand of the Majesty on high.' Most people only know Christ as dying on the cross. They go to the cross and think of his blood, his love and his atonement. This has an influence upon them, and they get truly converted. Their conversion is brought about by God's Spirit. But this is only the first, preparatory stage of Christ's work in their lives. Then there is the second, higher part of his work, and that is his reign of power in the glory of heaven. Oh, dear Christian friends, the holy God who lives in heaven wants us to live heavenly lives. We have a heavenly calling, and we cannot live in a heavenly atmosphere unless we have the very life of heaven in our hearts. That is why Jesus, after he was crucified on earth, was exalted into the glory of heaven, so that from there he might bring heavenly joy, purity and blessing into our hearts. Is that not what we long for? Is it not what we need?

You may have often bowed at the foot of the cross and yielded yourself to Christ, knowing that you are purchased by his blood and conquered by his love. And yet you have never been able to maintain your consecration or fulfil your vows. Why is this? The reason is not that you have stood too much by the cross. No; but at the cross you have looked too much at the cross itself instead of at the Crucified One, who is now living and acting in the power of the heavenly life. You have not understood and believed that the loving Redeemer who died for you also possesses the very omnipotence of God and can pour a heavenly life into your heart.

It is this knowledge of Jesus in his heavenly glory and power which is the key to the teaching of the Epistle to the Hebrews, and the key to the Better Life which it holds out to us. The soul who sees Christ in his heavenly, kingly power, who believes that by the Holy Spirit he can and will keep us in full fellowship with himself, who really knows that Jesus is at the right hand of the Majesty on high, has the secret of the Second Blessing.

The history of Israel

Our third illustration is taken from the history of Israel. The relevant passage is Hebrews 3:7–4:14. The two stages of their history after they had been redeemed from Egypt come out very clearly here. The first stage is the wilderness, into which God brought them so that they might see his wonders and learn to trust him. They were to enter into a covenant with him and then prove their allegiance to him by letting him lead them into Canaan. This was to be the second stage. They had left Egypt simply to escape from the suffering and bondage to which they had been subjected there. Before they entered Canaan they were to have the opportunity of showing that they were prepared to do it of their own free will, content to be led by God into the promised land. Their gaining possession of their inheritance was to be an act of faith and obedience. It was God's will that they came into the wilderness; it was his will that they should only stay there a short time, just long enough to show that they were ready to pass through it and out of it at God's bidding. But Israel failed sadly.

We have here a picture of the two stages of the Christian life. At conversion many Christians are simply moved by the instinct of self-preservation: they want to escape the wrath to come. They do not understand that they have been called to a life of entire devotion to Christ. So God allows them to enter the wilderness of failure and want, so that they may come to recognise their own weakness, learn to trust him and prove that they are ready for an intelligent and wholehearted acceptance of all that he offers them. Like Israel, most Christians fail. Because of their unbelief and disobedience they do not receive the full blessings which God has in store for them. They do not really experience the fulfilment of all that God has promised. They wander in the wilderness for forty years. They never know what it means to enter into Canaan – the life of peace, victory and abundance. Passing out of Egypt through the Red Sea is the first blessing; entering Canaan through the River Jordan is the second.

There is nothing more convicting in all of God's Word than the third and fourth chapters of Hebrews, and at the same time there is nothing more encouraging. These chapters show us the reason for our passing through the wilderness, for our experiencing failure and weakness. We know something of God and have experienced his power and grace, and yet we know we are not living in the fullness of God's promises. The reason for this is quite simply our lack of obedience and faith. However, the Epistle also assures us that 'we which have believed do enter into rest' (4:3). There is a life in which the rest of God fills the soul, in which the soul is made more than conqueror over every enemy.

This is the Second Blessing. We see here the great lesson which we drew from our second illustration and which is evident throughout the whole Epistle – we see that it is through the knowledge of Jesus that this blessing comes. *He is our Joshua.* He has the power to lead us into the rest of God. If we have not yet experienced this, it is simply because of our unbelief. We have not trusted him to bring us in and keep us there. He has said to us, 'Go up, possess the land,' but because of our unbelief we have disobeyed him. We have not surrendered our lives to him so that we may live by his strength alone and do his will alone. We are grieving him by our wilderness life. We even doubt whether the life in Canaan is better than the life in the wilderness. Let us yield to Jesus; let us trust him. Joshua brings us into the promised land. He turns every promise into experience.

The state of the Hebrews

The state of the Hebrews to whom the Epistle was written was very similar to that of their fathers in the wilderness. In their condition we find our fourth illustration of the two stages of the Christian life. The writer was about to describe the spiritual glory and heavenly power of our Lord Jesus as Melchizedek, but having mentioned that name he then interposes a long parenthesis of warning and rebuke to his readers (5:12-6:20). He says he is afraid that they are utterly unfit to take in the wonderful truth he wishes to teach them. He contrasts what they are with what they ought to be. They are 'dull of hearing'. They still need to be taught the basic truths of the Christian faith, even though, having been Christians such a long time, they should by now be ready to teach others those truths. They are like babies needing milk, rather than full-grown men able to enjoy solid food. Their spiritual sense should have been developed by use so that they could now discern good from evil, but instead they are 'unskilful in the word'. They are content to be always preoccupied with foundational truths such as repentance and faith, resurrection and judgement; they know nothing of pressing on to perfection in the Christian life.

There is insufficient space here to go into all the wonderful meaning which the word 'perfection' has in this Epistle. However, since the writer says, 'Let us go on unto perfection', and we read so much about Christ having been perfected and having perfected us, we may be sure that we are meant to understand that our perfection is in Christ. He makes us partakers of his own perfection. We can have the full experience of what Jesus in his perfect, heavenly glory can do for us and in us.

It is not that the Hebrews are not intelligent or clever enough. Rather, they are carnal – their hearts are wrong and incapable of appreciating spiritual truth. They have been converted, but have made no progress: their lives have been at a standstill, without growth. They have been wandering in the wilderness.

This is the Second Blessing, when a soul comes to see and confess the wrongness and wretchedness of the life it has led, and yields to Jesus so that he can do more in it than it has yet known. The realisation of the need for change and still more the entrance into the enjoyment of the Second Blessing has been to many a believer, even more remarkably than his conversion, like passing from death to life.

The priesthood of Christ

We find our next illustration in the priesthood of Christ, as typified by Aaron and Melchizedek. We look upon Aaron, the high priest of Israel, as a wonderful type of Christ, and we do so rightly. And yet when in Psalm 110 God speaks of the everlasting priesthood of his own Son who is to come, he says that he will not be a priest in the order of Aaron but in the order of Melchizedek. The great secret which this Epistle unfolds – the great secret of the Christian life – lies just in correctly understanding this difference between Aaron and Melchizedek.

And what is the difference? We read of our blessed Lord: 'He was crucified through weakness, yet he liveth by the power of God' (2 Cor. 13:4). In Aaron we see the former half of this truth, in Melchizedek the latter; in Aaron Christ's earthly work of propitiation and the purging away of sin; in Melchizedek the work in heaven, in the power and life of the eternal world. In Aaron's work we see wonderfully expressed the great truths of blood-shedding and atonement, of representation and acceptance in another, who can sympathise with us and act on our behalf. But Aaron teaches us almost nothing about what takes place within the veil after the blood has been sprinkled and about the life of the one who has been accepted in God's presence. Aaron can afford us only the slightest glimpses of Christ's resurrection power, of his sitting at the right hand of God, of his dispensing the power and the life and the joy of his own heavenly glory to his people on earth. His priesthood was a fallen and human one; he died himself, and his sons died. The everlasting, unchanging life-power in which Christ was to minister the blessings of the heavenly sanctuary had to be typified by another. And so Christ became a priest in the order of Melchizedek.

Melchizedek was not only a priest but also a king. He was the king of righteousness and the king of peace. In him priesthood had realised its ideal. He sat upon a throne and so could bless in power. His priesthood was royal and it was unchanging and everlasting. We read of none from whom he received it and of none to whom he gave it up. He 'abideth a priest continually' and is the type of the Son of God, who saves in 'the power of an endless life' (Heb. 7:16). Melchizedek teaches us that it is with a kingly power that Christ can now work, since he is seated upon the throne on the right hand of the Majesty on high. His power is unfading, continuing everlastingly from moment to moment. It is the power of eternity.

A believer experiences the Second Blessing when, pressing on to the perfection that is in Jesus Christ, he begins to see what Christ as his Melchizedek can be to him. As long as I only look to Christ as my Aaron, as long as I only look to the cross and to the blood shed on earth, I can never attain to the full experience of the power of an endless life. But this Epistle teaches me to look upward and to base my expectations upon what my Lord is and has for me in heaven. It says to me: 'We see not yet all things [subject to] him, but we see Jesus ... crowned with glory and honour' (Heb. 2:8–9). It tells me: 'Of the things which we have spoken, this is the sum: We have such an High Priest, who is set on the right hand of the throne of the Majesty in the heavens' (8:1). Out of heaven and in heavenly power our great High Priest brings to us the blessing of the Most High God. As we learn to know him in this, his saving power; as we learn to yield to him not only as Priest but also as King; as we trust the power of the endless life in which he works and through which he can maintain our life in us, we see how true is the teaching of this Epistle – that the understanding of the Melchizedek priesthood is hidden from the slothful, carnal Christian, and is the one thing we need to lead us on to perfection in Christ Jesus.

It is in the light of this truth that that wonderful verse which expresses the practical application of Hebrews chapter 7 gets its full meaning: 'Wherefore he is able also to save them to the uttermost that come unto God by him, seeing he ever liveth to make intercession for them' (7:25). Jesus can save me 'To the uttermost' – that is, completely, because he 'ever liveth', moment by moment, to pray for me and to impart to me what he receives from God in answer to his prayers. His unceasing, never-failing life-intercession is the secret of my unceasing, never-failing life of salvation. Why is it that my pulse never for one moment fails or stops? Because my heart does not for one single moment stop sending out its living streams. And why is it that my spiritual life need never for one moment fail or stop? Because in the heart from which the Holy Spirit comes there is never one moment's intermission; from the loving heart of my Lord Jesus there goes up to the Father an unceasing stream of intercession, and there comes down to me an unceasing stream of blessing. Jesus is always praying for me. He is able to save me completely, because he is the High Priest in the power of an endless life. To live in the truth of this is to have the Second Blessing.

The Better Covenant

This Epistle is throughout a comparison of the two stages of man's relationship with God, as seen in God's dealings with man, in Christ's work for man and man's own experience. We should notice that the word *better* is very frequently used to describe the second stage. It is found thirteen times in the Epistle and is one of its key words. We may very justly call the true Christian life to which the writer of the Epistle wished to lead the Hebrews the Better Life. In this connection there is one more illustration of the two stages which we should look at. In chapter 7 we are told that Christ has become the Mediator of a better covenant, established on better promises. God had said in the prophecy of Jeremiah (31:33–34) that he would make a new covenant. It would not be like the covenant he had made with Israel in the past. Even though that covenant had been made by God himself, it had to pass away. It had only been intended as a preliminary, as a preparation for something better. It was a training school in which the people were to learn and appreciate their utter weakness and helplessness. Through the Old Covenant the people were to gain the desire for God's full salvation and the will to accept it.

In the New Covenant that full salvation comes to us with its threefold blessing. The first part of the blessing is such a complete and real forgiveness of sins that God can say, 'I will remember their sin no more.' God also says, 'I will put my law in their inward parts, and write it in their hearts.' By his Holy Spirit God will place in our hearts the law of love for God and his will. Then God's love for us and ours for him will be able to meet. As a result of this we will know God: 'They shall all know me.' Perfect fellowship and direct, immediate communication between God in heaven and my soul here below will be established. Oh! When I truly and fully come out of the Old Testament life into the New, a blessing comes into my soul which is nothing less than the love and presence of God in the living Christ. This is the Better Covenant. This is the life that Jesus, as the Mediator of the Better Covenant and the minister of the Heavenly Sanctuary, can give to and keep in all those who trust him. Many Christians who, like the Hebrews, have come under the New Covenant, are still living the life of the Old, with all its feebleness and failures. May God bring us all to fully believe that there is a Better Life, a Heavenly Life, received in Christ, our high Priest in the Heavens.

These illustrations of the Second Blessing in the Epistle to the Hebrews all show clearly that in the relationship between God and man, man's weakness demands that there should be two stages – a stage of preparation and a stage of fulfilment. We can also see that man sins when he rests content with the preparatory stage longer than God would have him do so, instead of pressing on to perfection. What is known as the Second Blessing is the experience of the second stage in the life of the Christian. Then the soul comes into direct personal relationship with God in Christ and fully apprehends and receives the heavenly work of Jesus in its divine power and fullness. The soul enters into the rest of God and reaches true maturity in the Christian life, in conscious union with Christ in his glory and tasting the perfect fulfilment of the New Covenant promise.

In conclusion I would like to make one more point. In our blessed Lord Jesus a wonderful life of faith, obedience, rest, victory, joy and strength has been prepared for us Christians. And it is all to be found in the knowledge of what Christ is, in the power of his endless life. We need to get our eyes, our hearts and our faith fixed on him as he sits at the right hand of God, watching over us, imparting to us and maintaining within us the eternal life which God intends his children to live on earth. And how do we obtain the fullness of this eternal life? We must always come back to the old answer, which is the surrender and obedience of faith.

A surrender is needed. If I want the life of heaven – as much of the heavenly life as my Lord in heaven can give – I must give up the life of earth. If I want the life of Christ in me, I must give up the life of self. There must be very real and entire surrender. I need to give up and turn away from the way I have lived as a Christian in the wilderness if I am to enter into the rest of God, the heavenly life of my Lord within the veil. I need to have an attitude of perfect and entire obedience to God's will. And that can only come through faith. The whole of the eleventh chapter of Hebrews is one great witness to faith as the secret of all God's dealings with men, the one source of their obedience to him and their acceptance by him. We must learn to gaze on Jesus in faith, to listen to Jesus, as God speaks him out of his heart into our hearts. We must let Jesus in his heavenly glory become our life. Then he will do for us more than all we can ask or think.

Christians, are you ready or this? Ready to give up everything so that Christ may dwell in you, so that God may fill you? If we are ready, if we are truly thirsty for Christ, he will satisfy our thirst and will reveal himself to us in the power of his endless life.

Chapter 2

Have You Received the Holy Spirit?

Paul said unto them, 'Have ye received the Holy Ghost since ye believed?' Acts 19:2

There was once a professor who discovered that for a long time he had been making a serious mistake in the way he had been teaching his students. He had taken every possible trouble to explain to them the problems which came up in the course of their studies, but he had often found that he could not hold their attention. He asked himself what the reason might be, and he concluded that it was because he had not allowed them to try and solve those problems themselves. They had never clearly recognised the difficulties which existed and which had to be overcome. And so he decided to try another method. He now took great pains to make the problems involved in each exercise plain to them, and then he let them attempt to think them through themselves and seek a solution. The students would usually get stuck, and then the professor's own solution was always welcome and clearly understood.

I find that a similar situation exists with the preaching of God's Word. Preachers tell people about the great redemption of Christ, but if they have never known what it is to be sinners and how deeply they have fallen, the preaching of redemption is almost meaningless to them. It has no interest for them for the simple reason that they have no sense or feeling of the necessity of that redemption. This is the reason why throughout the Church of Christ there is so much profitless preaching.

Just as many of the unsaved are unaware of their need for salvation, so too many Christians are unaware of their need to receive the Holy Spirit. This was the case with the twelve believers whom Paul met at Ephesus. They had been baptised and had professed their faith in Christ. No doubt they were honest, upright, earnest men. But when he talked to them Paul very soon saw that they lacked something, so he asked them, 'Have you received the Holy Spirit?' They answered, 'No, and to tell you the truth, we don't understand what you're talking about. We have not heard about the Holy Spirit.' 'What have you been baptised into, then?' asked Paul. 'John's baptism,' they answered. 'That's very good, as far as it goes,' said Paul. 'You're right to believe that Jesus was the Messiah who was to come, and that he died, but there is a great deal more to it all than that. Jesus rose again after he died, and he has fulfilled his promise that his Holy Spirit would come down.' Once he had told them this, they were ready and willing to be baptised in the name of the Lord Jesus. And yet even this was not enough. Paul then laid his hands upon them and they received the Holy Spirit. And they began to speak in strange tongues, which was one of the manifestations of receiving the Spirit in those days.

The first lesson

This conversation in the book of Acts teaches us some very important lessons. The first is that the most necessary thing in the Christian life is to receive the Holy Spirit. Let us try to understand why this is so. You may say, 'But surely we have received the Holy Spirit. Why do you question that? How can a man be converted without the Holy Spirit?' But I am not here talking about conversion. The expression 'receiving the Holy Spirit' does not refer to that secret working of God's Spirit by which a person is brought to salvation. Receiving the Spirit is something which occurs after conversion. The Holy Spirit does indeed work in the hearts of the unconverted and struggles with them, convincing them of sin and pointing them to Jesus. But the Spirit only works in such hearts – he does not stay in them. The Spirit works in the heart of every man who is converted, but he does not necessarily live there and take up his abode and dwell there. After conversion and baptism into the name of Jesus, believers still have to receive the Holy Spirit. Why is this so? This points us back to what Jesus taught his disciples.

We have the clearest indication of what receiving the Holy Spirit was in the case of the twelve apostles. They were with Jesus for three years. Every day he taught them, and they enjoyed a wonderful personal relationship and fellowship with him. And yet we know how unsanctified they were and how they grieved the Master by the weakness and the lack of love which they displayed. But he said to them, 'The time is coming when everything will be changed. I have promised my Spirit, and when you receive him you will know that I am in my Father, and you are in me, and I am in you, even nearer than I now am upon earth.' So the Holy Spirit came down at Pentecost. And what did that mean? It meant that by the Spirit Jesus could live in them and enable them to live in a new way. Before Pentecost Jesus was outside of them, external to them. During the three years of his earthly ministry, he exercised a great influence over them. But he was not where he wanted to be – in their very hearts. What he wanted to do for them was to make their hearts like his, full of humility, gentleness and love. And so he was always pointing them to a better time, and it began with the day of Pentecost. So an outward Saviour became an inward Saviour. He took possession of the disciples and came and dwelt in their hearts. His character, will and aims became their own.

Why is there so much complaint in the Church of Christ about spiritual feebleness, instability and backsliding? The answer is this: Christ is so often preached about and experienced only as an external Saviour. Preachers talk about Calvary and the Ascension, and yet many believers say, 'Oh yes, I have an almighty Jesus up in heaven, but there seems to be a distance between him and us. We want to feel him nearer.' Why do they feel this way? Because they do not know him as an indwelling Saviour. The Holy Spirit has come to accomplish just that for us. Jesus said, 'He shall glorify me in you,' and by that he did not mean that God was merely going to give us glorious ideas about his Son. The soul cannot feed upon ideas. I want bread. You may tell me about the nature and essence of bread, but that does not feed me. I want the bread within me. And so Christians too often try to feed upon the words of God while forgetting that the living Christ must be an inward Saviour.

In effect Christ said to his disciples, 'You may not dare to preach until you have received the Holy Spirit.' The Holy Spirit was not just an idea, but a reality. And so today no one should dare to speak of the redeeming power of Christ without an inward experience of him in their heart and soul. If we would only live as God would have us live, our work for the Lord would exercise a mighty influence. Our lives, our conversations, our prayers and our whole faith would have a strong power over people and would proclaim that Jesus is not merely an outward Saviour but, through the Holy Spirit, is an inward one.

The second lesson

When Paul met these twelve believers at Ephesus he found them to be honest, earnest men. However, although they were believers in Jesus, they knew only half the truth about him. They had not received the Holy Spirit. So we have seen that the one thing which every Christian needs is to receive the Spirit. This leads us on to our second main point, namely that there may be a great deal of very earnest religion in our lives without our ever having received the Spirit.

A person may even be happy as a Christian for a time without receiving this gift of the Holy Spirit. In Acts chapter 8 we read that Philip went and preached in a city in Samaria. Great numbers of people there believed and were baptised, and there was great joy in the city. News of this came to the Apostles in Jerusalem. They realised that the Samaritans were lacking something, so they sent two of their number to them. When they arrived in the city the very first thing they did was to call the people together to teach them, pray with them and lay hands on them. They received the Spirit, and so enjoyed the full blessing of the Christian dispensation.

The fact that it is possible to be a sincere Christian without having received the Holy Spirit presents us with a great problem in the Church of Christ. If one were to ask the majority of Christians, 'Have you received the Holy Spirit since you believed?' they would almost have their breath taken away by the question. Of course, they would not answer, 'I have never heard about the Holy Spirit,' because he is mentioned quite often. But they might say something like, 'I don't understand what you mean. What does it mean to receive the Holy Spirit? Didn't I receive him when I received Jesus?' Oh, believe me, there is a great difference.

We often hear complaints about the state of the Church. People say that the Church is not what it should be, that there is a widespread spirit of worldliness and a lack of commitment, that there is too much dependence upon tradition or preaching, while in the relationships between Christians there is an absence of the close fellowship of the Spirit which should exist. You may hear about Holiness Conventions or about full salvation and the deeper spiritual life. Some of you may say, 'I can't understand what this is all about.' Really the whole issue boils down to this question: 'Have you received the Holy Spirit?' We need to receive the Spirit so that the life of Christ may enter us and live in us fully.

The third lesson

The third main point which I wish to make is that the greatest aim of the Christian ministry ought to be to bring people to the Holy Spirit. Someone might argue, 'Isn't there a danger here of leading people away from the grace of God in Christ and encouraging them to look into their own hearts too much?' It would certainly be a grave mistake to preach Christ and the Holy Spirit as two separate Saviours, but a minister is not preaching the full gospel if he preaches Christ without also stressing the need to receive the Holy Spirit. Receiving the Spirit means that the living, heavenly, glorified Jesus comes and dwells in our hearts. People sometimes wonder if the Spirit is some kind of substitute for Jesus, since Jesus said, 'I will go away, and send the Holy Spirit.' But the

Spirit did not come as a replacement for Jesus but rather to bring Jesus closer to us than ever – even closer than he was to the disciples on earth. So the great work of the ministry ought to be to bring the knowledge of the Holy Spirit to believers. Paul asked the Corinthians, 'Know ye not that ye are the temple of the Holy Ghost?' The spiritual life of the whole Corinthian church was feeble because they had no knowledge of the Holy Spirit.

And so we should all pray and wait upon God, and set our hearts and our faith upon this gift that the Father gave to the men of Ephesus, so that we too may be filled with the Holy Spirit. Oh, brother, sister, are you earnestly seeking and crying to him so that you may get filled with the Spirit? The question is often asked, 'How can I receive the Holy Spirit?' You can only receive him through prayer. You must receive him personally from God. God must speak. You may have heard a great deal of good advice on the subject. People may say that in order to receive the Spirit, the believer must search his heart and part with all sin. Others may say that you must have a very simple faith in Christ's promise of the Holy Spirit. All this is very true, but there is something even more important. Quite simply, we must get the Holy Spirit from God himself. We must feel our own powerlessness, and in humility before God, we must let him do his work. There will have to be a personal dealing with God. There must be a very full opening of the heart itself to God. There will have to be prayer, and prayer will have to be the very spirit of our lives. We should constantly be saying, 'I want this one thing, O God: to be filled with the Holy Spirit.'

Are you ready to say, 'O my God, I thirst for you'? Surely that is not too much to say in order to receive the Holy Spirit and his mighty power to reveal Christ. Let us say it and say it with our whole heart. But remember, it is a very serious thing to say, 'I am now going to be a vessel set apart for the Holy Spirit to dwell in, to rule and guide me as he pleases.' Perhaps you may think, 'Ah, that is too difficult for me in my circumstances.' Brother, the Holy Spirit is the living God, and he brings the joy of God, the love of God and the Son of God himself into your heart. Don't be afraid. Make the sacrifice.

I plead with you, Christians, even though you may not understand it all very clearly – say to God, 'You have something for me, your child, which I have never before had. There is a blessing I have never before understood or received. I will cry for it. I will wait for it.' Child of God, however ignorant you feel about it, begin by saying trustingly, 'My Father's love for me is greater than my love for him.' You are longing earnestly for the Spirit, but he is knocking at you door even more earnestly. Take him in, in faith, and say, 'Blessed Father, are you willing to live in your child and completely fill him with your Spirit? Come into me and rest in me.' Trust God and wait day by day for this change to happen. It may not necessarily be the case that a long wait is needed, but if it is, be patient, depending on your God.

Have you received the Holy Spirit since you believed? Every child of God ought to give an answer to this question. Do you know what it is to have received the Holy Spirit as the indwelling life of Christ, as the revealer of Jesus, as the communicator of the power of God? If not, then I ask you, do you desire to receive him? Oh, the Church of Christ would be very much the better and so would the world if God's people would only believe his Word and receive his Spirit. May God help us and make us all to receive himself. Amen!

Chapter 3

The Promise of the Holy Spirit

> *If ye then, being evil, know how to give good gifts unto your children: how much more shall your Heavenly Father give the Holy Spirit to them that ask him?* Luke 11:13

Here we have a revelation of the heart and will of God in heaven. What is God's attitude towards us? What view should be have of him when we come to him in prayer? In what light should we look upon him? Let us look upon him as a Father ready to give a great gift to every one of us. There are some gifts which God does not give, and some prayers which he does not answer, but there is one prayer he will always answer – and that is a prayer for the Holy Spirit. Let us look up to God. He is willing, waiting, longing and able to give us his Holy Spirit.

What is there in the child of God which corresponds to this great purpose of the Father? In the child there is hunger. And what attitude should each of us have when we pray? We should have a great, longing desire for the Holy Spirit and a willingness to receive him. Is there a longing for the Holy Spirit in our hearts? We need to pray, 'O God, since you are my Father and I, your child, am ready, give me the Holy Spirit.'

We may desire the Holy Spirit and God may be ready to give him to us, and yet there may be a great deal that hinders us from receiving him. This truth is expressed in Ezekiel 36:25–27: 'Then I will sprinkle clean water upon you, and ye shall be clean: from all your filthiness, and from all your idols, will I cleanse you. A new heart also will I give you: and I will take away the stony heart out of your flesh, and I will give you a heart of flesh. And I will put my spirit within you.' How clear that is! How simple! God cleanses away the filthiness and the idols; God takes away the hardness of heart that the world instils in us, and then he gives us the Holy Spirit. So the first thing we need in order to receive him is deliverance from sin.

When the Holy Spirit comes he comes to take complete control: he comes to control the whole of our lives. He does not merely want possession of the minister in the pulpit, or of believers when they are going out to evangelise or do some special task for the Lord. Rather, the Holy Spirit comes to dwell, to stay, to rule, to control. Let us pray, 'Lord God, cleanse me from sin, and accept my total surrender to the control of the Holy Spirit.'

We are looking and longing for the Holy Spirit; our desire may be vague and indefinite or it may be very specific. But somehow we do not receive what we long for. However, when we accept God's claim to the lordship of our lives and submit to it and yield ourselves to the control of the Holy Spirit, then we just need to believe and trust, and we shall receive. Perhaps our faith may be tested by a prolonged wait or by difficulties, but let us believe that God will satisfy our desire for his Spirit.

I cannot think of anything which I find more wonderful and instructive than the ten days of praying and waiting which preceded the outpouring of the Holy Spirit at Pentecost. It is a mystery, and I cannot understand it. Jesus had died upon earth and had conquered sin; he had been raised from the dead, lifted up to the Father's throne and glorified; he had received the Holy Spirit from the Father so that he could give him to the believers. And yet despite all this there were ten days of waiting in heaven. God was ready, Christ was ready, the Holy Spirit was ready, the Trinity was ready – and yet for ten days the Spirit could not come. Why? Because there had not been enough prayer. Jesus had spent three whole years preparing those disciples and everything was ready in heaven, and yet those ten days of prayer were still needed.

Everything in heaven is ready even now. God is ready – he wants us to receive him as our Father. Christ the Son is ready – his work is finished and he longs to prove to us how complete our redemption and acceptance are. And the Holy Spirit is ready to take possession of us in the name of Jesus, so that he may glorify Christ.

But are we ready? And will our prayers be proof that we are ready? Our prayers should express our desire for more grace in order that we might bring blessing to others. We should long for more of that quiet power of Christ within us which witnesses to people even when we are not talking about him. You know how Peter spoke to the lame man at the temple gate. He did not preach a sermon to him. Instead he told him, 'Such as I have I give thee: in the name of Jesus Christ of Nazareth rise up and walk.' He was saying, 'I know Jesus, and the power of

Jesus, and I will give that to you.' Like Peter, we want to say, 'I know Jesus. He has done so much in my life, and he will do it for you.' That is the sort of power we need to have. How do we get this power? By surrender to the Holy Spirit. All our prayers, all our searchings of heart and all our believing must come to this – Jesus Christ by his indwelling Holy Spirit must have complete possession of us. Then we shall be clean, sanctified vessels, ready for the Master's use.

So we are hungry and thirsty. There is only one thing which can satisfy us, and we should be prepared and willing to give everything to obtain it. It is the presence, the rule, the control and the power of the Holy Spirit.

Let us listen to our Redeemer as he speaks to us: 'If ye then, being evil, know how to give good gifts unto your children, how much more shall your heavenly Father give the Holy Spirit to them that ask him?' Let us look up to God upon his throne, expecting the Holy Spirit, and let our hearts have a deep desire, a deep childlike surrender, and a deep, deep trust in God's almighty power.

Chapter 4

Keeping the Full Blessing of Pentecost

> *Praying in the Holy Ghost, keep yourselves in the love of God ... Now to him that is able to keep you from falling ... to the only wise God our Saviour, be glory ... now and forever. Amen.* Jude 20, 21, 24–25

Can anyone who has had the full Pentecostal Blessing lose it? Without a doubt he can. God does not give this blessing with such force that people must keep it whether they are willing or unwilling. The blessing is given to the believer like a talent which should be used and looked after and which can bring happiness only by being used. Just as the Lord Jesus, after being baptised with the Holy Spirit, had to be made perfect by

obedience and subjection to the guidance of the Spirit,
so the Christian who receives the Pentecostal Blessing
has to take care that he looks after what has been given
to him.

Scripture shows us that we can only keep the blessing
we have received by entrusting it to our Lord for safe
keeping. Paul wrote to Timothy, 'He is able to keep that
which I have committed unto him ... That good thing
which was committed unto thee keep by the Holy Ghost
which dwelleth in us' (2 Tim. 1:12, 14). Jude advises his
readers, 'Keep yourselves in the love of God ... [who] is
able to keep you from falling.' What we must do is to be
humbly dependent upon the Lord who keeps us and
through whom alone we are able to retain the blessing.
As with the manna in the Old Testament, so too with this
blessing: it must be renewed from heaven every day. Just
as our bodies must inhale fresh air from outside us every
moment, so our spirits must inhale the Holy Spirit. Let
us see how this everlasting, uninterrupted keeping of the
blessing is achieved.

Jesus, who gave us the Blessing, will maintain it for us

Jesus is the Keeper of Israel: that is his name, and that is
his work. God has not only made the world: he also
keeps and maintains it. Jesus not only gives the Pentecostal Blessing: he maintains it continuously. The
Holy Spirit is not a mere power which is subject to us and
which we can make use of. He is a power who is above us
and over us, who governs us and works in us, by whom
Jesus in heaven continues his work from moment to
moment. We ought to have an attitude of the deepest
dependence upon God, fully aware of our nothingness
and powerlessness. Our great work is to allow Jesus to
work in us.

As long as the soul does not understand this, it will
always feel some dread of receiving the full blessing: 'I

will never be able to maintain such a holy life,' it says. 'I will not be able to remain on such a height all of the time.' These thoughts show how little the soul understands the subject. When Jesus comes by his Holy Spirit to dwell in the heart, to live in me, then he will really do that, and take charge of my whole life. Life lived in the Pentecostal Blessing is a life of joyfulness: that joy is watchful, but it is also carefree. The Lord has entered the heart, his temple; he will dwell there and do everything. He asks only one thing: that the soul will know and honour him as its true Shepherd and its Almighty Keeper. So we can see that Jesus, who gives the Pentecostal Blessing, will certainly keep it in us.

Jesus maintains the Blessing, just as he gave it, through our faith

'According to your faith be it unto you' is the prevailing law of the Kingdom of God. The believer's faith, which when he received the Lord Jesus as Saviour was only like a small mustard seed, must extend itself during the progress of the Christian life, so that he may see and receive and enjoy more of the fullness that is in the Lord. Paul wrote, 'I am crucified with Christ: nevertheless I live; yet not I, but Christ liveth in me: and the life that I now live in the flesh I live by the faith of the Son of God' (Gal. 2:20). His faith was as multi-faceted and incessant as the necessities of his life and work were. In every situation and need, and without exception, he trusted in Jesus to do everything. He had given his life to Jesus: he did not live anymore. By a continual and unlimited faith he allowed Jesus to do his perfect will in his life.

The fullness of the Spirit is not a gift that is given once for all as a part of the heavenly life. Rather, it is a constantly flowing stream of the river of the water of life which issues out of the throne of God and of the Lamb. It is an everlasting communication of the life and the love of Jesus, a most personal and heartfelt involvement of the loving Lord with his people on earth. In those who understand this and consent to it and hold fast to it with joy and with constant faith, the Lord Jesus will most certainly do his work of maintaining the blessing.

Jesus maintains the Blessing if we seek communion with him

The only purpose of the Pentecostal Blessing is to manifest Jesus in us as Saviour, in order that he may manifest his saving power in and through us to the world. The Spirit did not come instead of Jesus, but only and wholly in order to make the disciples more intimately and perfectly in relationship with the Lord than they had been when he was on earth. The power from on high did not come as a power which they could consider as their own: that power was bound inseparably to the Lord Jesus and the Spirit. Every action of the power was an immediate action of Jesus in them. All the aspects of the relationship which the disciples had had with Jesus when he was on the earth – following him, receiving his teaching, doing his will, sympathising with his suffering – were to continue even more powerfully, since through the Spirit the life of Jesus was now inside them. And it is the same with us. The Spirit in us will always glorify Jesus, always show that he alone must be Lord, that everything that is beautiful comes only from him. We must be faithful in seeking his words and his will in Scripture, in sacrificing effort and time we could spend with other people in order to spend time with him, if we are to keep the blessing. Jesus wants us to occupy ourselves wholly with him. Anyone who loves communion with Jesus above everything else will find that he will maintain the Pentecostal Blessing in him.

Jesus maintains the Blessing if we are obedient

When the Lord Jesus promised the Holy Spirit, he said three times that the blessing was for the obedient soul: 'If ye love me, keep my commandments. And I will pray the Father, and he shall give you another Comforter' (John 14:15; see also 14:21, 23). Peter spoke of 'the Holy Ghost, whom God hath given to them that obey him' (Acts 5:32). Of our Lord himself we read that because he was 'obedient unto death … God hath highly exalted him' (Phil. 2:8–9). Obedience is what God must demand; it is the only right attitude of creature to Creator, and also the only way to salvation for the creature. It was what was lost in the Fall, and it was what Jesus came to replace. It was the very essence of the life of Jesus. Without it the Pentecostal Blessing, which is the life of Jesus in us, cannot be obtained or maintained.

There are two kinds of obedience. There is a very defective type, as exhibited by the disciples before the day of Pentecost. They longed to do what the Lord commanded, but they lacked the power. And yet graciously Jesus accepted their intention to obey as obedience. And there is also a deeper form of obedience which comes with the fullness of the Spirit, through which the believer is given the power to obey fully. So in order to retain the fullness of the Spirit we must be obedient to God even in the smallest things. In everything we do we must listen to the voice of Jesus, to the voice of the Holy Spirit. This is the way in which Jesus wants us to live, because it was the way in which he himself lived. Being obedient to the Father as he was is the way to ensure that the Pentecostal life in us is constant and permanent.

The practice of this obedience gives the soul a marvellous frankness and firmness and a power to trust God and expect everything from him. Knowing that we can trust God to provide all our needs if we are obedient gives us the strongest possible incentive to do his will faithfully.

Jesus maintains the Blessing if we share it with others

When the Christian begins to seek the full Pentecostal
Blessing, he often thinks only of himself. Even when he
receives the Blessing he is at first inclined to see how he
can keep it safely for his own benefit. But the Spirit will
soon teach him that a member of the Body of Christ
should not try to enjoy the Spirit of that Body in separa-
tion from the other members. He begins to understand
that there is only one Spirit and only one Body. He must
cherish the unity of the Body if he is to enjoy the fullness
of the Spirit.

   This truth teaches us very important lessons about the
conditions on which the blessing, once received, can be
kept. Everything that you have belongs to the others and
must be used for their service. Everything they have
belongs to you and is indispensable to you. The Spirit of
the Body of the Lord can work powerfully only when the
members work together. You must confess to others
what the Lord has done for you, ask for their intercession, seek fellowship with them and help them by using
the gifts which the Lord has given to you. You will take
deeply to heart the state of backslidden or misguided
Christians whom you know – but not in a spirit of judgement or bitterness, but rather in one of humility and
prayer, kindheartedness and readiness to serve. Jesus
will teach you the wisdom and blessedness of a loving
attitude, and as you sincerely surrender to your fellow
Christians he will maintain and deepen the Pentecostal
Blessing in your life.

Jesus maintains the Blessing for the good of his Kingdom

The Spirit came as power to work. The life of Jesus was
one of entire consecration to God's work, of complete
commitment to the purpose of saving souls. For this
object alone he lived and died; for this cause alone he

lives in heaven. How, then, could anyone think of having the Spirit of Christ except as a Spirit dedicated to God's work and the salvation of souls? So we must remember that the Spirit works in us in order that he may work through us. Our seeking for the Blessing will not succeed, our original possession of it will be lost, if we do not place ourselves at the disposal of the Spirit so that he may do his work through us. Anyone who is willing to work as God directs and not according to his own will, who submits himself to the Lord and waits for him with an undivided heart, will find that working for the Kingdom, far from exhausting or weakening him, is the sure way of keeping the treasure of the Pentecostal Blessing.

It is as the indwelling Lord that Jesus maintains the Blessing in us

Christ does not dwell in us in the same way as we live in a house. Rather, he indwells us in the way that the soul lives in the body, giving life to every part of it, being one with it. The indwelling Christ penetrates our whole nature with his nature. This is the reason why the Spirit came to make him present in us. As the sun is high above me and yet penetrates by its warmth into my marrow and bones and warms my whole body, so the Lord Jesus, who is high in heaven, penetrates my whole nature with his Spirit in order that all my willing, thinking and feeling may be animated by him. Through the Pentecostal Blessing our relationship with Jesus is no longer with an exterior Person in heaven but with One who dwells in the heart and fills it in a divine and all-pervasive way. So we can see how natural and certain it is that Jesus will maintain the fullness of the Spirit within us, since he himself lives in us.

Do you long for the fullness of the Pentecostal Blessing and yet fear to enter into it because you cannot imagine how you will persevere in it? Oh, listen – Jesus himself will make that blessing continual and certain. Do you long for the blessing and yet cannot understand the secret of it? Listen – the secret is that Jesus Christ will become your life and will live his life in you by his Spirit every day. Nobody can understand what it is like on the top of a mountain until he has been there. Although you cannot understand everything, do believe that the Lord Jesus has sent his Spirit with no other purpose than to take possession of you in his divine power and to keep the fullness of the Spirit in you. So trust in him. Let go of every doubt and difficulty and receive from him that full Pentecostal Blessing as a fountain, which he himself will cause to spring up in you into everlasting life.

Chapter 5

The Holy Spirit and Money

*All that believed were together, and had all
things common; and sold their possessions
and goods, and parted them to all men, as
every man had need.* Acts 2:44–45

When the Holy Spirit came down at Pentecost to dwell in
men, he assumed the charge and control of their whole
lives. They were to be or do nothing that was not under
his inspiration and leading. In everything they were to
move and live and have their being 'in the Spirit', to be
wholly spiritual men. So it necessarily followed that their
possessions, property and money were also to be subjected to his rule, and their income and expenditure
were to be governed by radically new principles. In the
opening chapters of Acts we find several illustrations of
the Holy Spirit's all-embracing claim to guide and judge

in money matters. Acts has much to teach us about the place which money should have in the individual believer's life and in the life of the Church.

The Holy Spirit taking possession of money

'All that believed were together, and had all things common; and sold their possessions and goods, and parted them to all men, as every man had need' (Acts 2:44–45). 'As many as were possessors of lands or houses sold them, and brought the prices of the things that were sold, and laid them down at the apostles' feet: and distribution was made unto every man according as he had need. And ... Barnabas ... having land, sold it, and brought the money, and laid it at the apostles' feet' (4:34–37). Without any command or instruction, in the joy of the Holy Spirit – the joy of the love which had entered their hearts, the joy of the heavenly treasures which now made them rich – the believers spontaneously parted with their possessions and placed them at the disposal of the Lord and his apostles.

It would have been strange if it had been otherwise, and a terrible loss to the Church. Money is the great symbol of happiness in this world; one of its chief idols, drawing men away from God; a never-ceasing temptation to worldliness to which the Christian is exposed every day. A salvation which did not give the people complete deliverance from the power of money would not have been a full salvation. The story of Pentecost assures us that when the Holy Spirit comes in his fullness into the heart, then earthly possessions lose their place in it and money is only valued as a means of proving our love and doing service to our Lord and our fellow men. The fire from heaven which consumes our whole lives as we offer ourselves to God as living sacrifices also consumes our money, turning it into altar gold, holy to the Lord.

We learn here the secret of Christian giving, and indeed the secret of all true Christian living, and that is the joy of the Holy Spirit. Sadly, this joy is often lacking in our giving to God. Often habit, the thought of duty, human argument and motive and a feeling of the need around us have more to do with our giving than does the power and love of the Spirit. Such motivations are necessary and right in their proper place, of course. The Holy Spirit makes use of them in stirring us to give. There is a great need for developing firm principles and fixed habits of giving. But what we need to realise is that all this is just the human side of the matter, and by itself it cannot be adequate if we are to give in the measure and spirit which makes our every gift a sweet-smelling sacrifice to God and a blessing to our own souls.

There is universal complaint in the Church about the terrible need for more money for God's work and about the shameful disproportion between what God's people spend on themselves and what they devote to their God. The pleading cry of many of God's servants who work for the poor and the lost is often heart-piercing. We need to take to heart this solemn lesson: all this is simply a proof of the limited measure in which the power of the Holy Spirit is present among believers. We should each fervently pray that our whole life may be so full of the joy of the Holy Spirit, so absolutely yielded to him and his rule, that all of our giving may be a spiritual sacrifice through Jesus Christ.

The Holy Spirit dispensing with money

'Then Peter said, "Silver and gold have I none; but such as I have I give thee: In the name of Jesus Christ of Nazareth rise up and walk!"' (Acts 3:6). We have already seen that money may be both a sure proof of the Spirit's mighty working and a blessed means of opening the way for his yet fuller activity. But there is always a danger here. Men begin to think that money is the great need; that an abundance of money coming into the Church is a proof of the Spirit's presence; that money must be strength and blessing. However, as the verse quoted above shows, the power of the Spirit can in fact be displayed where there is no money at all. The Holy Spirit is the mighty power of God, sometimes condescending to use the money of his saints, at other times proving how divinely independent he is of it. The Church must allow God to enable her to grasp the double truth that while the Holy Spirit claims all her money, his mightiest works may be achieved without it. The Church must never beg for money as if it were the secret of her strength.

The Apostles Peter and John were in the earthly sense penniless, and yet precisely because of their poverty they were all the more able to bestow heavenly blessings. They were poor, and yet they made many rich. Where had they learned this? Peter says, 'Silver and gold have I none; in the name of Jesus Christ, walk.' These words point us back to the poverty in which Christ had commanded them to live and of which he had set them such a wonderful example. By his holy poverty he had shown men what a life of perfect trust in the Father was; how the possession of heavenly riches made a person independent of earthly goods; how earthly poverty qualified a person for holding and giving out eternal treasures. The inner circle of his disciples discovered his power by following in the footsteps of his poverty. The Apostle Paul was taught the same lesson by the Holy Spirit. He seems to say in his letters that to be always in eternal things, free even from lawful earthly things, is a wonderful, almost indispensable help in witnessing to the absolute reality and sufficiency of the unseen heavenly riches.

We may be sure that as the Holy Spirit begins to work in power in his Church, we will see him working mightily as he takes possession of his people. Some will by their giving make themselves poor, having a living faith in the inestimable worth of their heavenly heritage and being filled with the fervent joy which the Spirit gives them. And some who are poor and in acute need as they work for God will learn to cultivate more fully Peter's joyful attitude: 'Silver and gold have I none; but such as I have I give thee: in the name of Jesus Christ, walk!' And some who have not been called to give everything will then give with a new generosity, because they begin to see the privilege of giving all, and long to come as close to it as they can. And we shall have a Church which gives willingly and abundantly, and yet does not for a moment trust in its money, instead honouring above all those who have the grace and strength to be followers of Jesus Christ in his poverty.

The Holy Spirit testing money

'Barnabas ... having land, sold it, and brought the money, and laid it at the apostles' feet. But a certain man named Ananias, with Sapphira his wife, sold a possession, and kept back part of the price, his wife also being privy to it, and brought a certain part, and laid it at the apostles' feet' (Acts 4:36—5.2). Ananias brought his gift, and with his wife was struck dead. What made the gift such a crime?

He was a deceitful giver. He had kept back part of the price. He gave with half a heart and unwillingly, and yet wanted the credit for having given everything. In the Pentecostal Church the Holy Spirit was the motivator of the giving, so Ananias' sin was against the Spirit. No wonder it is written twice in this passage, 'Great fear came on all them that heard these things' (5:5, 11). If it is so easy to sin even in our giving, if the Holy Spirit watches and judges us as we give, we may well be fearful.

What was Ananias' sin? Simply this: he did not give all

he professed to give. This sin does not usually occur in
such a blatant form as in the case of Ananias, but in a
more subtle form it is far more common than we might
like to admit. There are many who say they have given
their all to God, and yet they prove that this is not so by
their use of their money. There are many who say that all
their money is the Lord's and that they hold it as his
stewards, to dispose of it as he directs them, and yet by
the amount they spend on God's work, compared with
what they spend on themselves and on saving for the
future, they prove that in their case stewardship is just
another name for ownership.

Without being exactly guilty of the sin of Judas,
Caiaphas and Pilate, who crucified our Lord, a believer
may nevertheless associate himself with them by the
spirit in which he acts. We may condemn the sin of
Ananias, but we may still be grieving the Holy Spirit by
sinning as he did, withholding from God what we have
professed to give him. Nothing can save us from this
danger but a holy fear of ourselves and a very full and
honest surrender of all our opinions and arguments
about how much we possess and how much we give to
the testing and searching of the Holy Spirit. Our giving
must be in the light if it is to be in the joy of the Holy
Spirit.

And what was it that led Ananias to this sin? It was
probably the example of Barnabas; he did not wish to be
outdone by another. So often we ask ourselves what men
expect of us! What people will think of us is usually more
at the forefront of our minds than what God will think of
us. And we forget that God counts our gifts only according to how the heart gives: it is the wholehearted giver
who pleases him. Sadly, the Church has done much to
foster the worldly spirit that values gifts by what they are
in men's sight rather than by what they are in the sight of
the One who searches the heart.

May the Holy Spirit teach us to make every gift part

and parcel of a life of entire consecration to God. We cannot give in this way until we are filled with the Holy Spirit.

The Holy Spirit rejecting money

The case of Simon the sorceror is just as sobering as that of Ananias. 'Simon offered them money, saying, "Give me also this power, that on whomsoever I lay hands, he may receive the Holy Ghost"' (Acts 8:18–19). But Peter replied, 'Thy money perish with thee, because thou hast thought that the gift of God may be purchased with money' (verse 20). The attempt to gain power or influence in the Church of God by money brings perdition.

Here, even more than with Ananias, the problem was simply ignorance of the spiritual and unworldly character of the Kingdom of Christ. How little Simon understood of the men with whom he was dealing! They needed money for themselves and others. But the Holy Spirit, and the power and treasures of the unseen world, had taken such possession of them and had so filled them that money was as nothing to them. They would rather it was destroyed than it should have anything to say in God's Church. They would rather let it perish than for one moment encourage the thought that the rich man can acquire a place or a power which is unavailable to the poor man.

Has the Church been faithful to this truth by standing courageously against the claims of wealth? Sadly, history shows that she has not. There have been a few noble Christians who truly lived out the apostolic teaching that the gift of God is superior to every earthly consideration. But too often the rich have been given honour and influence in the Church, regardless of their spiritual worthiness. This has surely grieved the Spirit and harmed the Church.

We need to apply all of these thoughts to our own

lives. Our nature has been so brought under the power of the spirit of this world, and our fleshly mind, with its attitudes and habits of thought and feeling, is so subtle in its influence, that nothing can deliver us from the mighty spell of money but a very full and lasting experience of the Spirit's presence and working. Only the Holy Spirit can make us entirely dead to all worldly ways of thinking, and he can only do this by filling us with the very power and life of God.

Let us pray that we may have such a faith in the transcendent glory of the Holy Spirit and in his absolute sufficiency as the Church's God-given strength and wealth, that money may always be kept under Christ's feet and under ours, of worth only as the earthen vessel for his heavenly ministry.

Blessed Lord Jesus, teach us and keep us so that like Barnabas, we may lay all our money at your feet and at your disposal. Teach us and keep us so that like Peter, we may rejoice in the poverty which teaches us to prove our trust in the power of your Spirit. Teach us and keep us, so that we may avoid the sin of Ananias, so that our giving to you does not belie our profession of living entirely for you. Teach us and keep us so that we may avoid the sin of Simon, so that we do not presume that your gifts and power over men can be obtained by money.

Most blessed Spirit, fill us with yourself! Come and fill your Church with your living presence, so that all our money may be yours alone. Amen.

Chapter 6

Consider Jesus

*Wherefore, holy brethren, partakers of a
heavenly calling, consider the Apostle and
High Priest of our confession, even Jesus;
who was faithful to him that appointed him,
as also was Moses in all his house.*
Hebrews 3:1–2

Consider Jesus: these words may be taken as the motto
of the Epistle to the Hebrews. The weakness of the
Christian living which the writer saw among the Hebrews and their danger of missing God's promises
through unbelief and disobedience was due to their
ignorance of the real nature of the perfect redemption
which had been offered to them in the gospel. If they
could only know Christ Jesus and what he could do for
them as their compassionate, Faithful, Almighty High

Priest, then their living would be in perfect correspondence with their beliefs and with the will of the Saviour whom they would then truly know.

Consider Jesus is the writer's one exhortation throughout this Epistle. In the first chapter he urges his readers to consider Jesus in his divine glory and power. He is the very image of God's substance and upholds everything by the word of his power. He does this in the natural world as the Son of God; how much more will he do it in grace for those for whom he came into the world, so that he might cleanse them from their sins. As the Son of God he is greater than the angels; how much more effective will be what he is and does for those who trust him than all that the angels did for God's saints in times gone by. Consider Jesus the Mighty God.

In the second chapter the writer depicts Jesus' humiliation, his 'partaking of flesh and blood'. In every way he was made like us; he suffered and was tempted, so that he might be a merciful and faithful High Priest. Consider Jesus, your Brother, the Suffering One, the Merciful One.

The Epistle then goes on to show how Jesus is greater than Moses and Aaron, the two bearers of the Old Testament revelation to Israel – Moses was the Apostle or Messenger, Aaron was the High Priest. In the first verses of the third chapter the writer shows us that Jesus, as the Son of God, is greater and worthy of more glory than Moses. So if Moses was faithful to God, how much more was Jesus faithful to his Father. Consider Jesus, the Faithful One, infinitely trustworthy, and learn to count on him to do all that he has undertaken to do.

Then in the fourth and fifth chapters we have the further opening up of the sympathy of Jesus as the Merciful High Priest, 'who can bear gently with the ignorant and erring' (5:2, RV) because he himself, in his days as a man, had to pray with pain and tears and learn obedience from what he suffered. If we are to hold fast to our

faith, if we are to come boldly to the Throne of Grace, if
we are now, 'even as the Holy Ghost saith, Today' (3:7),
to enter the Rest of God, it must all come through one
thing: looking to Jesus. Consider Jesus as the Merciful
High Priest until your heart is filled with his sympathy
and compassion, and it becomes impossible to doubt
that he will save you completely, even though you may
be ignorant and erring.

And then comes the Epistle's wonderful revelation of
the Melchizedek priesthood of Jesus, which he carries
out 'in the power of an endless life' (7:16). After this has
been expounded in chapter 7, it is summed up in chapter
8: 'Now ... the chief point is this: We have such a high
priest, who sat down on the right hand of the throne of
the Majesty in the heavens, a minister of the sanctuary,
and of the true tabernacle ... the mediator of a better
covenant' (verses 1–2, 6). Then the writer explains the
blessings of that covenant (chapter 8) and the power of
the Blood by which it was sealed, and through which the
entrance of the High Priest into heaven in order to
appear before the face of God for us was achieved (chapter 9). He gathers up all these truths in the words, 'By
one offering he hath perfected for ever them that are
sanctified' (10:14) and concludes, 'Having an high priest
over the house of God, let us draw near' (10:21–22). Our
whole spiritual life, the cleansing of our conscience, our
priestly service before the living God – all this depends
on one thing, and that is our knowledge of Jesus in his
heavenly priesthood. He calls us to live a heavenly life
here upon earth in divine power and in God's presence
and glory. The one thought of this Epistle, and of all of
God's gospel, and the one cure for all the feebleness and
failure of the Church and of our lives is this: *Consider
Jesus*.

What does the word 'consider' mean in this context? It
means to look at a thing from every side until you enter
into its true meaning and nature, until you master it and

all its secrets are opened to you. Remember, it is not reading this wonderful Epistle or knowing the Bible which will help you. It is something else; it is *Considering Jesus*. Consider Jesus until you have begun to know him personally and you have your heart filled with the thought of his priesthood and the three wonderful attributes of it which Hebrews expounds. Consider Jesus the Merciful High Priest, Jesus the Faithful High Priest, Jesus the Great High Priest in the power of the endless life. Consider Jesus until doubt passes away and confidence and fullness of faith and hope possess you, and your heart opens to receive him as a complete, ever-present, indwelling Saviour.

Chapter 7

We See Jesus Crowned with Glory and Honour

*But now we see not yet all things put under
him. But we see Jesus, who was made a little
lower than the angels for the suffering of
death, crowned with glory and honour.*
Hebrews 2:8–9

What a glorious contrast! We do not yet see all things
subjected to him – that is, to Man – but the wonderful
truth is that we see Jesus crowned with glory and honour. When we look around upon this world, with all its
sin and misery, it does indeed not appear as if Man were
destined to be higher than the angels and to have domin-
ion over all the works of God's hands. But Jesus became
a man that he might taste death for all men, and now he,

a man, sits upon the throne in heaven as our representative, our Redeemer, our Head. So it is enough for us that we see *him* crowned with glory and honour, because in that we have a pledge that he will one day bring Man to that same glory and honour; in that we have the assurance that he is even now using all that glory and honour on our behalf.

The right understanding and use of this antithesis is the secret of the life of faith. 'We see not yet all things put under him' – how exactly this expresses the disappointment and failure which is so often the experience of the believer when his first joy and hope has begun to pass away. He finds that sin is stronger than he had guessed; that the power of the world and the flesh and self are not yet subjected to him as he had hoped they would be. At times he almost feels that the promises of God are untrue and that the expectations which they raised in his heart were false. Or else he may acknowledge that God does indeed faithfully fulfil his promises (which is the right attitude for someone in his circumstances) and he finds most precious God's promises to make him more than a conqueror, and yet time and again he has the bitter experience of discovering that all things are not yet subjected to him.

Blessed is the man who knows how to say with living faith, 'But we see Jesus crowned with glory and honour!' Blessed is the man who knows how to look away from all the imperfection and failure in himself and to look up and behold all the perfection and glory which is to be found in Jesus. Blessed is the man who finds his delight and his life in meeting every difficulty and disappointment by looking upon Jesus, the One who is crowned with glory and honour. That is all we need! It satisfies the soul and gives it peace and joy and strength.

Chapter 8

Today

Wherefore, even as the Holy Ghost saith,
'To-day if ye shall hear his voice, harden not
your hearts.' Hebrews 3:7

These words are generally applied to the unconverted. However, the Psalm in which they originally appear and the context in which they are quoted in this Epistle both prove that they are meant for God's people. In all the dealings of the Holy Spirit with believers, whether they are weak and erring or strong and glad, his great word to them is 'Today'.

What does this mean? God is the Eternal One. With him there is no yesterday or tomorrow; what we call past and future are with him an ever-present Now; his life is an ever-blessed, never-ending Today. One of the great words used in this Epistle with reference to Christ and his salvation is the word 'eternal'. He has become the author of eternal salvation – that is, of a salvation which bears the mark of eternity. Its chief characteristic is that it is an ever-present Now; there is not a moment in which Christ, who always lives to pray for us, is not able to maintain that salvation in us in the power of his endless life.

Man is the creature of a moment: the past is gone from him, and he has no control over the future. It is only the present moment that is his. That is why, when he puts his faith in Christ, who is a High Priest forever, and receives the eternal salvation which he gives, God's great word to him is 'Today'. In Christ all the blessedness of the great eternity is gathered up in an ever-present Now. The one need of the believer is to know this, to respond to it, to meet the 'Today, Now, my child!' of God's grace with the 'Today, even Now, my Father!' of his faith.

The Holy Spirit says, 'Today', and yet Satan's word is always 'Tomorrow'. It is man's favourite word as well. The child of God who has unbelief in his heart will also say it. He finds God's demand too great for today; God's promise is too high; he hopes it will be easier for him later on. But the same Holy Spirit who says 'Today' to us is also the Mighty Power of God who is himself ready to do in us everything that God wills and asks. Every moment the Spirit is pleading with us to surrender immediately, to trust God right now, and he possesses the power to realise all of God's promises in our lives.

'Today': it is a wonderful word of promise. It says that today, at this very moment, the amazing love of God is for you; at this very moment it is waiting to be poured out into your heart. All that Christ has done and is now doing in heaven, and all that he is able to do in you, is within your reach this very day. Today the Holy Spirit, in whom there is the power for us to claim and enjoy all that the Father and the Son are waiting to bestow – today the Holy Spirit is within you, sufficient for every need, equal

to every emergency. With every call to full and entire
surrender which we find in our Bibles; with every promise we read of grace for the meeting of earthly and
spiritual needs; with every prayer we breathe and with
every longing in our hearts, there is the Spirit of Promise
whispering, 'Today'.

'Today': it is a word of solemn command. We are not
here talking about some higher privilege which you are
free to accept or reject. Believer, it is not for you to
choose whether or not you will receive the fullness of
blessing which the Holy Spirit offers. His 'Today' brings
you under the most solemn obligation to respond to
God's call and to say, 'Yes, Lord, today I submit completely and immediately to all your will; today I surrender in present and perfect trust in all your grace.'

'Today': it is a word of serious warning. 'The Holy
Ghost saith, "Today, if ye shall hear his voice, harden
not your hearts."' He has said of those who ignore his
'Today', 'They shall not enter into my rest' (Heb. 3:11).
There is nothing so hardening as delay. When God
speaks to us, he asks for a tender heart, open to the whis-
pers of his voice of love. The believer who answers the
'Today' of the Holy Spirit with a 'Tomorrow', hoping for
some more convenient time, does not understand how
dangerously he is hardening his heart. The delay,
instead of making the surrender and obedience and faith
easy, makes it more difficult. It closes the heart against
the Comforter today and cuts off all hope and power for
growth in the future. Believer, when you hear his voice
today, open your heart with great tenderness to listen
and obey; obedience to the Spirit's 'Today' is your only
certainty of power and blessing.

For all Christians whose lives have been characterised
by feebleness and failure, who have not yet entered into
God's rest, this word 'Today' is the key to all their disappointments and to all their hopes. You waited for
strength, to make obedience easier; for feeling, to make

the sacrifice less painful. You did not listen to the voice of God, breathing through every word he speaks, even through the Living Word, Jesus Christ, that wonderful note of hope – 'Today'. You thought it referred to the calling of a sinner to repentance; you did not know that it is meant for the believer, that it is a command to immediate, wholehearted submission to all that God says each time the believer hears his voice, a call to immediate, trusting acceptance of all that he gives.

In the Epistle to the Hebrews we have a wonderful explanation of what Christ, as a High Priest at the right hand of God, can do for us in the power of his endless life. Our entering into the rest of God, the perfect cleansing of our consciences in the blood through which he entered into the presence of God, our entering within the veil into that presence, our being brought close to the very heart of God, our being taken up and kept in Christ in the love of God – these blessings are all ours. And over each of them is written the words, 'Now, today, is the accepted time.'

Brother, you and I should bow in great stillness before God to hear this wonderful message: to hear the Holy Spirit whispering, 'Today, Today'. Let us open up our whole hearts to take it in. Let all fear and unbelief pass away as we remember that it is the Holy Spirit himself – the giver of strength, the dispenser of grace, the revealer of Jesus – who says 'Today'. Let our faith simply listen to God's voice, until it rings through our souls day by day and all the day. We shall take God's Today and make it our own. We shall meet this wonderful Today of God's love with the confident Today of our faith. And it will become to us a foretaste of that eternal Today in which he dwells. The Holy Spirit's Today, accepted and lived in, will be within us the power of an endless life, the experience of an eternal salvation as an ever-present, never-ceasing reality.

'Even as the Holy Ghost saith, "Today"…'

Chapter 9

Able to Save Completely

> *Wherefore also he is able to save to the*
> *uttermost them that draw near unto God*
> *through him, seeing he ever liveth to make*
> *intercession for them.* Hebrews 7:25, RV

The translation, 'able to save to the uttermost' is one
which perfectly expresses the sense of the original. However, its meaning is often misunderstood. 'To the uttermost' does not refer to time, to the end of all things. Nor
does it refer to the depths from which Christ saves, to his
ability to save even the vilest and those farthest away
from God. The true meaning is to do with the thorough
working out of salvation in those who have already been
saved. The verse means, 'Christ is able to save in every
way, in all respects, *unto the uttermost*; so that every
want and need, in all its breadth and depth is utterly

done away' (Delitzsch). He is able to save completely.

This power to save is connected with his always living to pray as our eternal High Priest. There are two elements in the concept of the eternal life of Christ. One is that of unbroken continuity, the other is that of infinite power. The heavenly life of Christ knows no break or change, no fading or failing for one single moment, and its every present instant is filled with the life of the eternal Now. And he sits at the right hand of the Majesty on high, with all the limitless power of God. The words, 'he ever liveth to make intercession' teach us that the eternal life which he lives is just one unceasing, uninterrupted prayer for us and an unceasing, uninterrupted receiving from the Father of the answers to his prayers. He carries out his priestly intercession in 'the power of an endless life' (7:16).

Here lies his power to save completely. Just as there ascends from him moment by moment a continuous, all-availing intercession, so there returns from the Father to him, in an unbroken stream, the Spirit and the life and the grace which his praying always secures; and from him all these blessings descend to us. It was an eternal salvation of which he became the author; it was an eternal redemption which he obtained for us; it is an everlasting priesthood which he ministers in the heavenly sanctuary; it is in unbroken continuity that Jesus is able to save. This is what Scripture means when it says he is able to save completely, because he always lives to pray. His prayer is unceasing, and so is his salvation.

If we ask what the great complaint of believers is, and what the essence of their failure to experience their complete salvation is, we find that it is simply that their spiritual life has so many breaks and interruptions. The question which has proved to be the turning point in the life of many of God's saints has been this: Do you enjoy uninterrupted communion with God? It is a question which has searched many a heart which would have liked to say 'Yes' but dared not. *Uninterrupted communion with God*: this is complete salvation; it is the experience that the salvation is eternal, continuous, indissoluble. Christ's never-ceasing intercession is the power behind this constant communion with God. When Jesus said to Peter, 'I have prayed for thee, that thy faith fail not' (Luke 22:32), it was before his heavenly priesthood in the power of the endless life had been inaugurated; the Holy Spirit, who is that power, had not yet been given. But now, because Jesus always lives to pray for us, our faith need never for a moment fail. The weakness of the Old Covenant was that its priests 'by death [were] hindered from continuing' (7:23, RV). There was no continuity because their lives were not eternal: the eternal life was not yet revealed. 'But he, because he abideth [or continueth] for ever, hath his priesthood unchangeable. *Wherefore* also he is able to save to the uttermost [or completely] all who draw near unto God through him' (7:24–25, RV).

We read elsewhere: 'he that cometh to God must believe' (11:6). It is the person who draws near to God by faith in this ever-living and ever-praying High Priest, this Priest in the power of an endless life, who will experience the reality of the promise, 'He is able to save completely.' First there must be the faith which sees that this complete salvation is indeed prepared and secured in Christ: that his Spirit will maintain a faith which never fails, because Jesus always prays. Then follows the surrender – a very solemn and heart-searching act – surrender in order to be a completely saved man, always living, every moment, in the power of Christ's endless life, as one who is kept from falling by the unceasing intercession of the eternal High Priest. And then comes the appropriating faith, which having seen what God has prepared and having yielded wholly to Christ so that he may do his work, now claims and accepts the blessing. This is the faith in the One who is seated at the right hand of the Majesty on high, in our Priest-King, who saves and reigns in eternal power. This is the faith which is 'the substance of things hoped for' (11:1) and which makes the eternal life an abiding, unchanging experience.

Believer, Jesus lives in ceaseless intercession for you, without one moment's break, so that your faith will not fail, so that you may have uninterrupted communion with God. Do you enjoy such a communion?

Chapter 10

Drawing Near to God

> *Wherefore ... he is able to save to the uttermost them that draw near unto God through him, seeing he ever liveth to make intercession for them.* Hebrews 7:25

We all know the difference between a means and an end. A means never terminates in itself; it is subordinate to the end, which is the only reason for its existence. It is merely the way, which loses itself in the end, its goal and object.

Christ is not the End but the Way. He came to reveal the Father, to bring us 'unto God', to open a way in which we could draw near to God. Many Christians regard Christ as the End: if they have found him they are content. They do not understand that to have found Christ is just the beginning: the true End is to know God, to have communion with him, to serve him, to receive the manifestation of God himself in one's soul. This knowledge of God is given to those who cannot rest content without it.

The question may be asked, What is the difference between drawing near to Jesus, who is God, and drawing near to God? The answer is twofold. For one thing, in Jesus the divine has been clothed in human garb, and so it is hard to be sure how far it is really the divine in Jesus which attracts us. For another, in Jesus the divine grace and mercy is above all revealed, so in him we are all too apt to be seeking only our salvation, while we profess to be seeking God. The true test of the reality of our turning to God, the proof that we are not merely seeking salvation, is this: that we prize Christ and his work because *he brings us to God,* because in him *we draw near to God.*

Drawing near to God does not merely mean a nearness to God in theory, but an actual enjoyment and experience of that nearness – it means truly knowing the fellowship and presence of God and having uninterrupted communion with him. God made man for himself, to be his companion and his delight, to be the sharer of his thoughts and plans, of his love and glory. Through his sin man put self in the place of God, and so Jesus came to repair the damage which sin had done. He began the work by offering himself to God; he continues it by bringing us to God, so that we may offer ourselves to him; he perfects it when he leads us within the veil to the life of eternal nearness to God.

I wish that all of God's redeemed people really believed that such a life is possible, that the Holy God, who is all light, all love and beauty, is able to manifest himself to the soul in such a way that it always consciously lives in his presence. I wish they really believed that God, the hidden but Almighty One, has the power to act upon the soul of his child and fulfil the promise that 'We will come unto him, and make our abode with him' (John 14:23). I wish they really believed that in a divine and supernatural way which surpasses all understanding and which is above all that we ask or think, the soul can learn to know the love of Christ and be filled with the fullness of God. I wish they really believed that the Living Way, the way into the Holiest, has been opened up, so that we can truly enter and dwell there.

What new zest it gives to our hope in Jesus when we come to understand that this nearness to God is what he will give us. He has not only given us the right to come near to God, but also the power to do so – his Endless Life Power, which lifts us up and brings us into the Father's presence. We begin to see that it is not merely to be justified or sanctified, not only to be made happy or fruitful, that we must look to Jesus, but also for something far higher and more blessed. We must expect him to take us by the hand and bring us near to God, so that we may have lasting fellowship with him and experience his revelation of himself to our hearts. Oh, this is something more than the peace and joy which some Christians know at times. This is unspeakable joy in Christ, full of glory; this is the fullness of joy, the joy which no man can take from you.

In his book, *Three Friends of God*, Dr Tauler wrote:

All that God does for us and all the hidden ways of God which no eye can see, are in order that he may bring us into the holy and blessed delight of His Presence; bring us into the great depth of love, into Himself, the unfathomable blessedness.

It is not reading of God, or hearing of Him, or knowing of Him by sense or reason, that will satisfy us; but it is in receiving Him, drinking deeply of the fountain that springs from the eternal depths – drinking from Himself, where He is, and none other. Thus doth the soul know God, and in a nearer and a better way than all the teachers can tell of Him. For there is a nearness wherein we lose ourselves, and God is all in all. This may come to us in one swift moment; or, we may wait for it with longing hearts, and learn to know it at last. It was of this St Paul spake, when he said that the thing which eye hath not seen, nor ear heard, nor heart conceived, God hath now revealed to us by the Holy Ghost. Oh, how great, how inexpressible, how blessed, how immeasurable is the gift of the Holy Ghost! The Holy Ghost prepares the home in which He comes to dwell. And He fills the home with Himself, for He is God.

This is the reason why Jesus may apparently, in our experience, be unable to save us 'to the uttermost', why he cannot save us completely: he does this only for those who want to draw near to God. May we all seek to understand that Jesus wants to bring us to his Father, and that he will not rest until God is all in all in us.

Chapter 11

Entering into the Holiest

*Having therefore, brethren, boldness to enter
into the Holiest by the blood of Jesus ... Let us
draw near.* Hebrews 10:19, 22

Enter into the Holiest. With these words the second half
of the Epistle begins. Up to now the teaching has been
mainly devotional. The writer has shown us the glory of
Christ's person and priesthood; of the heavenly
sanctuary which he, through his own blood, has opened
and cleansed and taken possession of for us; and of the
way of obedience and self-sacrifice which led him to the
throne. Now comes the practical part of the message.
Our duty to appropriate the great salvation which has
been provided is summed up in one thought: 'Having
boldness to enter into the Holiest ... let us draw near.'
Access to God's fellowship and presence, and the right

and the power to make that presence our permanent dwelling place, has all been provided in Christ. So let us draw near, let us indeed live there.

Enter into the Holiest. This is a call to the Hebrews to come out of their life of unbelief and sloth, a life which leads towards a departing from the living God, and to enter into the promised land, the rest of God, a life lived in his fellowship and power. This is a call to all lukewarm, half-hearted Christians to remain no longer in the outer court of the Tabernacle, content with the hope that their sins are pardoned. They should not even be satisfied with having entered the Holy Place and having there carried out the service of the Tabernacle – not while the veil still hinders full fellowship with the living God and his love. They are called to enter through the torn veil into the Holiest, or the Most Holy Place, into which the blood of Christ has been brought, and where he lives as High Priest. There they are to live and talk and work in the presence of the Father. This is a call to all doubting, thirsting believers who long for a better life than they have yet known to cast aside their doubts and to believe that Christ has indeed opened the way into the Holiest for each one of us. This is the salvation which he has accomplished and which he loves to give to us, so that we shall truly live in the full light of God's face.

Enter into the Holiest. This one short phrase expresses the fruit of Christ's work, the chief lesson of the Epistle, the one great need of our Christian lives and the complete and perfect salvation which God has given to us in Christ.

Enter into the Holiest. What Holiest? None other than the very same Holiest into which Christ himself entered through his own blood after he had torn the veil by his death; thus he appeared before the face of God on our behalf. That Holiest is Heaven itself. But Heaven is not a locality, distinct and separate from this earth; it is not limited in space and time. Nor is Heaven the same as the physical heavens above us, even though these manifest God's glory in a special way. The true Heaven is spiritual and is as omnipresent as God himself. Where God is, there is Heaven; the Heaven of his presence even includes this earth. The Holiest into which Christ entered and opened the way for us is the light of God's holy presence and love. It is the state of full and complete union with him, and it is inaccessible to the natural world. Into that Holiest the soul can enter by the faith which makes us one with Christ. The Holy Spirit, who first showed that the way into the Holiest was not yet open, through whom Jesus shed the blood which opened that way, who on the day of Pentecost witnessed in the hearts of the disciples that it was now indeed open, wants to show to us today what it means to enter into the Holiest and wants to bring us in. He lifts the soul up into the Holiest; he brings the Holiest down into the soul.

Enter into the Holiest. Oh, the glory of this message! For fifteen centuries Israel had a sanctuary with a Holiest of All into which, under pain of death, *no one was allowed to enter.* This showed in the clearest possible way that man could not dwell in God's presence and fellowship. And now, how changed everything is! There used to be a warning: 'Do not enter!' Now there is instead an invitation: 'Enter in!' The veil is torn; the Holiest is open; God waits to welcome you into his embrace; from now on you are to live with him. This is the message of the Epistle: 'Child, my Father longs for you to enter his presence, to dwell there, and never again to leave.'

Oh, the blessedness of a life in the Holiest! Here the Father's face is seen and his love is tasted. Here his holiness is revealed and the soul is made a partaker of it. Here the sacrifice of love and worship and adoration, the incense of prayer and supplication, is offered in power. Here the outpouring of the Spirit is experienced as an ever-streaming, overflowing river issuing from the

Throne of God and the Lamb. Here the soul, living in God's presence, grows into more complete oneness with Christ and conformity to his likeness. Here, in union with Christ, who intercedes for us unceasingly, we are emboldened to take our place as intercessors who can have real power with God and receive his answers to our prayers. Here the soul mounts upon eagle's wings, and its strength is renewed. Here we are given blessing, power and love, with which we can go out as God's priests and win a dying world. Here each day we can experience the fresh anointing of the Spirit, in whose power we can go out to be the bearers and witnesses and channels of God's salvation to men, the living instruments through whom our blessed King works out his full and final triumph.

Jesus, our great High Priest – let this be our life!

Chapter 12

By Faith We Understand

By faith we understand that the worlds have been framed by the word of God, so that what is seen hath not been made out of things which do appear. Hebrews 11:3, RV

'By faith we *understand*.' The seat of faith is not the understanding or the reason, but the heart. Once faith possesses and quickens the heart, it then acts through the understanding. Faith understands divine things; through faith we can have spiritual understanding.

The message of this passage is simply this: by faith we understand the difference between the seen and the unseen, as well as the connection between them. By faith we perceive the 'invisible things' which the pagans lost sight of – that is, the 'eternal power and Godhead' of God, which are clearly seen 'from the creation of the world' and which are 'understood by the things that are made' (Rom. 1:20). If our faith is to worship and work properly, it must truly learn this first lesson: the created order, instead of being a veil which hides God, can become to us transparent with the light of his presence.

The Bible begins with the account of creation. Similarly, the writer of the Epistle to the Hebrews begins his record of what faith does with creation. Before leading us through the history of faith in the kingdom of grace and the spiritual life, he shows us how faith recognises God in the kingdom of nature. 'What is seen' has its ground and root in the things which are not seen. The worlds around us have been framed by the word of God; we understand this by faith. Our whole relation to the world in which we live is a matter of faith – faith in the invisible foundation of all that exists, and faith in the One whose word brought it into existence.

No one should think that this faith in a creation out of invisible things and in God as the Almighty Creator is something which is found as a matter of course in all those who believe the Bible, and that therefore this is not a lesson that we especially need to hear. If someone possesses this faith, it is very often a faith of the head more than of the heart, an intellectual belief or assent rather than a living realisation. The greater part of our lives has to be spent in contact with and under the influence of external things. The world of the visible around us continually leads us away from God and his presence. What we truly need is to have the visible so identified with the invisible in our minds, and the material world with the God who formed it, that he can hide and yet reveal himself within it, so that what is seen shall to us be transparent with the things which are unseen. Then the world around us will not be a hindrance but a help in recognising and remembering God and the spiritual world.

When our Blessed Lord lived among us in the flesh, he gave us an example of what it is to live in the faith that behind all visible things there is an unseen Power ruling everything. In the sun shining and the rain falling on good and evil alike, in the growth of the lilies of the field and the feeding of the birds of the air, he saw God. The child of God who wants to cultivate the habit of faith, who wants to become strong in faith, following in the footsteps of the faith-heroes of chapter 11 of Hebrews, must begin here. He must not only seek a faith based upon God's special promises or concerned with spiritual needs. What he needs more is the deep, quiet and abiding faith which sees God every moment, because it has learned always to recognise the invisible world in what it sees. The God of Grace is also the God of Nature. He does not needlessly repeat his lessons: those who do not sincerely try to accept his revelation of himself in nature will most definitely suffer loss. The presence of God in nature makes it a book of parables, full of teaching and strength for faith.

Modern science has made wonderful advances in the discovery of the laws and causes through which things exist and act. However, science is unable to discover a first great cause in the universe, so as a result a materialistic outlook has infected the whole of our thinking and literature. God is either denied or forgotten. This tendency is so natural to the human heart that not one of us is free from it. To 'worship and serve the creature more than the Creator' (Rom. 1:25), to be under creation's influence, trusting and rejoicing in it, is the sin not only of the pagans but of every human heart. It is only when the believer makes this a matter of thought and study and waits for the Holy Spirit to reveal God to him through the creation that he will escape from the subtle but powerful influence which surrounds him.

Once he realises the danger of materialism, our text in Hebrews points him to Genesis chapter 1 for the teaching and nourishing of his faith. There he should seek to know his God. As he sees God calling forth heaven and earth out of nothing, let him worship the One from whom and through whom and to whom all things are. In him they subsist: where they are and act, there God is and acts. Let the Christian believe in the God who rules everything, who is constantly bringing things forth into being. Let him believe in the working of a God of infinite power, wisdom and goodness.

As he studies God's work of quickening, ordering and making beautiful the world in the course of six days, at each progressive stage calling forth new powers of life until all his plans are accomplished, let him believe in the God whose way is slow but sure, who knows his plans and takes his time completing them, who not only begins but ends. In this way he will learn the two great rules which faith always needs to live by. The first is to trust God even though he keeps himself hidden and unseen. The other is to trust God even though his works may to begin with appear imperfect, because he acts through the law of slow and patient growth, which is the law of all created existence. The believer needs to trust God in the present as he does his unseen work and to trust him for the future as the Faithful One. Then he will understand why faith is both the substance of the unseen and the evidence of the hoped for.

Before we go further into the eleventh chapter of Hebrews to study how faith acts and what glorious work it does, let us learn here what the secret root of all faith's power is. You may have often complained that your greatest hindrance in the spiritual life is the constant contact you have with material, temporal things. You think you would be better off if somehow this contact could be broken. However, the way forward is not to withdraw from the material world but to allow it to become your spiritual helper. Faith can enable you to do this. It rises above what is seen and reaches through to the things which are not seen. This is the very essence of faith. It recognises the presence and the power of God.

It fills the soul with the sense of God's presence in everything that exists or happens. It is the open eye which sees God everywhere and always.

It is here we must begin. We must not only seek to claim promises and to trust for blessing, to be stronger in faith for prayer and work; we need to know better, to be brought into more personal contact with, to have our whole being at every moment overshadowed by the presence which fills heaven and earth. Material things will then no longer be hindrances, but will instead be helps to the spiritual life, because faith will everywhere recognise on them the stamp of God the Unseen. When Jesus said, 'Ye believe in God, believe also in me,' he called on his disciples to transfer all their faith in the Unseen God of the Old Testament to himself as the Son of Man, God's revelation in the New. But we canot do this unless we first seek and possess what he meant by belief or faith in God.

Beloved believer! If you want to be strong in faith, begin at the beginning. Lay a deep foundation. Study what the word says about the God of Creation as a pledge of what the God of Redemption will do (see 2 Kings 19:15–16; Is. 40:26–28, 48:11–13; Jer. 32:17). Cultivate the habit of bowing in quiet worship and just seeking to understand that behind what is seen there are unseen things. You will then learn to be more occupied with and influenced by the unseen than the seen. You will learn to go through each day in the awareness of the presence and power of the Unseen God. Then your faith will find it easy to trust him for his every promise and for your every need.

Chapter 13

The Faith of Abel

By faith Abel offered unto God a more
excellent sacrifice than Cain, through which
he had witness borne to him that he was
righteous, God bearing witness in respect of
his gifts: and through it he being dead yet
speaketh. Hebrews 11:4, RV

Abel is the first figure to be depicted in this wonderful portrait gallery in Hebrews chapter 11. Since his example of faith is the oldest, it reveals to us the root and beginning and the real secret and very essence of all faith: that is, faith sacrifices. Sacrifice is the fullest expression not only of what faith sometimes does, but also of what it really and always is.

Faith means sacrifice. We are so accustomed to think of faith as the opened hand or heart which receives and takes in what God gives that we forget that faith in its deepest meaning consists of giving as well as receiving. In fact we cannot receive until we give, and we cannot receive more than we give. The reason why our faith so often fails in its attempts to receive is that it wants to do so without the giving. Faith means sacrifice: the going out of self, the giving up of self, in order to find one's hopes and life in another. The very first element of worship is sacrifice, because it is the simple and complete expression of what God claims, of our relation to him and our hope in him. As the life of faith grows stronger in us and its heavenly significance becomes clearer, we shall see that sacrifice is its strength and value. By faith we offer a sacrifice which is acceptable to God, and this assures us that we are righteous and pleasing in his sight.

Faith finds the lamb for the sacrifice. Why didn't Abel just bow before God and give himself to him as a living sacrifice? Why did he not simply, in an act of consecration and self-dedication, offer himself to the Lord, utterly and entirely? What prompted him to seek a lamb and shed its blood and lay its body before God to be consumed? The reason was this: Abel felt himself to be a sinner. He knew that his sinful life could not be a sacrifice which was acceptable to God.

Sin and death are inseparably connected. The death of the lamb meant confession and vicarious expiation of sin; atonement for and redemption from sin. By substituting the lamb for himself and its death for the death he had deserved, Abel was testifying that for a sinner the only way to God is through death. There is no way to deliverance from sin and its guilt and power, no way into the life of God, except through the death in which sin is atoned for and taken away.

And so our faith centres and rests in Christ, the bleeding Lamb of God. His death is at one and the same time the revelation of what sin is, of how its punishment is borne and of how its power is broken. Faith always presents Christ to God as the sacrifice of perfect obedience and infinite merit. Faith sees something of its divine power and everlasting effectiveness and loses itself in Christ; in presenting him to God the soul presents itself too. The true spirit of self-sacrifice and obedience always finds both its liberty and its power in the sacrifice of the Son of God, since his death to sin was the power behind his death for sin. And so his death for sin, with us and on our behalf, leads to our death to sin with him and on his behalf.

Faith unites itself in death with the lamb in the sacrifice. Abel not only gave up the lamb to death; soon afterwards he yielded up his own life. In a divinely symbolic way the death of the lamb opened up the way and proclaimed the need for his own death, since in a world of sin death is the only path to life. In a far greater way, as we seek to enter into the meaning and power of the death of Christ for us, we hear with ever greater clarity the call to die with him. The more intensely our faith lives on him, the sacrifice for sin, in spirit and in truth, the more the Spirit of Sacrifice takes possession of us. We see that to die with Christ, to be like the One who not only dies for sin but to sin, is the secret of the life of faith.

Faith penetrates through the visible into the invisible; by faith we understand that what is seen comes from what is unseen. Faith enters into the very spirit of the sacrifice of Christ Jesus; it appropriates and assimilates it; it sets its whole being open to its power; it denies self, takes up the cross, and follows Jesus. The blessed truth of Substitution is found to have both its root and its fruit in that of Identification; the unceasing sprinkling of the heart and of the evil conscience in the precious blood is the guarantee of the unceasing and ever-increasing action in us of the Eternal Spirit through whom Christ offered himself to God. Christ died for us so that we might die with him. The very essence of a full and growing faith is that we forsake everything, we lose our very lives, we become living sacrifices.

'*By faith Abel offered unto God a more excellent sacrifice ... through which [faith] he had witness borne to him that he was righteous.*' If we have this faith which lives in the sacrifice of Christ in its completeness as the source and the law of our lives, then we will receive from God the witness or assurance that we are righteous and pleasing to him. It is not possible that a soul should really give itself utterly to God, *in Christ,* without the Father then giving the soul the deep witness of his pleasure in the soul and his love for it. In Christ the Lamb there is perfect acceptance by God, assurance from God and fellowship with God.

'*And through it [Abel], being dead, yet speaketh.*' He not only received witness from God, but also bears witness for God. Although he is dead, he still speaks to us. He speaks not despite his death, but because of it; his death is the power of his witness. In Abel, in Christ, in every believer, it is the faith which sacrifices everything, which gives itself up to God even to the point of death, which speaks with power.

Believer, do you wish to speak for God as Abel does? Remember the lesson: by faith we sacrifice. By faith we enter into fellowship with the Crucified One. By faith we give ourselves to the death, and being dead, we speak. Faith gives up all its life and hope in order to find its life in Christ and his atonement. And then, having found its life in him, it lives like him in the power of his life as a sacrifice to God for men. And as it looks upon the power of sin around it, whether in the more immediate circle or in the wide world which is full of ungodliness and paganism, it casts away all that man would set store by and finds in Jesus Christ and his sacrifice its message and its law, its inspiration and its hope. Because faith lives in him it can speak and work under the impulse of his infinite sympathy for the perishing. The power of his love will win them, because his is a love which gives itself and even dies for them.

So sacrifice, the death of self, makes way for the life of Christ in us. Being dead, we shall speak.

Chapter 14

By Faith We Walk With God

By faith Enoch was translated that he should
not see death; and he was not found, because
God translated him: for before his translation
he hath had witness borne to him that he had
been well-pleasing unto God.
Hebrews 11:5, RV

In Abel we had a picture of faith approaching God,
yielding itself to him in the death of the lamb, which was
at the same time the atonement for sin and the expression of surrender. Abel received assurance that God
accepted this sacrifice and considered him righteous. In
Enoch we now see how this same faith manifests itself as
a walk with God: 'Enoch walked with God' (Gen. 5:22,

24). These few simple words reveal the deep meaning of the life of faith. Fellowship with God or walking with God is the ruling principle both of the inner life and of its outer expression. God himself is everything to the soul. We will now consider how we can obtain such a life.

Faith seeks the Divine Presence. When a friend invites me to take a walk with him and I call at his house for him, the one thing I want is himself. If he is busy, I wait for him. If he is not at home, and I am told where he can be found, I go and seek him: I want my friend himself. Without his presence, how could I walk with him? This is the great problem in the lives of many Christians: they lack a real, deep sense of the Holy Presence as a spiritual reality to be obtained every day and enjoyed all the day. Do you want to walk with God? Then each morning seek the personal Presence of your God.

Faith enables you to do this – not the faith which only thinks of asking and receiving, working and conquering, but the faith by which, in the death of Christ, the soul has entirely sacrificed itself to God, and now knows that it cannot and need not live one moment without him. In quiet worship and waiting, it looks up to him. It counts upon him to make himself known to his child. It opens its eyes and heart to receive the full reality of the One who is the Mightiest Power, the Most Impressive Object in the universe, and who in infinite love delights in revealing himself to those who seek him. Oh brother, let your faith day by day make this its first aim: to wait for and secure the full sense of the Holy Presence with you. Such faith will make the walk with God a blessed reality.

Faith trusts the Divine Guidance. On one occasion I took a walk with a friend in a strange place on a dark night. I knew neither the turnings which the path might take nor the difficult places where I might be in danger of stumbling. But as I took his arm and he assured me that he knew every step of the way, I dismissed all my fear and walked on with perfect confidence. A walk with

God appears to many believers like a walk in the dark. It is true that to our human understanding it is indeed a walk in darkness, but in reality it is a walk in the Light. The person to whom it looks dark, who fears and doubts the daily walk with God, wondering if it might be too high and too difficult for him, should remember that faith trusts in the Divine Guidance. He should cultivate a childlike belief that his Father loves to have his child walk with him, that he has promised to hold his hand and to give him all the strength he needs. Nothing pleases God so much as our unbounded trust that he will enable us to walk with him. Such faith receives the blessing for which it has trusted God.

Faith accepts the Divine Will. The story of Abel showed us that faith means sacrifice – the giving up of everything, even life itself, to receive a new life out of death. In the walk with God this faith is brought into daily operation. Two cannot walk together unless they are agreed about the direction they are to take. When an inferior wishes to walk with a superior, the will of the superior must rule. If I am to walk with God, I must first agree to go in the direction he wants. Faith looks for God's way. Faith studies and discovers his direction in his Word, in his providence and above all in his blessed Son, and it accepts his way and will implicitly. The faith which walks with God implies, in its very nature, the sacrificial, wholehearted and unhesitating acceptance of all his will, and the childlike teachableness which listens and learns in order to know what his will is and how to do it. By such a faith we walk with God.

Faith receives the witness that we are pleasing to God. I cannot enjoy a walk with a friend if I doubt whether my company is agreeable to him or whether my behaviour is acceptable. The real blessing of the child of God is this: not only does God love him with an infinite compassion, even when he is wayward and wrong, but he also loves him in a more positive way, because the attitude of the child's heart and the behaviour which springs from that attitude is pleasing to God. Many Christians think this is an impossible attainment; sadly, it will be unto them according to their faith. By faith Abel received the assurance that he was righteous, Enoch that he was well-pleasing to God. If we ask our Father for it, and tell him that we cannot rest until we know that we are well-pleasing to him, he will give us this assurance. This is just what he wants us to know and rejoice in: the assurance that he sees in us, as we live in Christ and are indwelt and guided by the Spirit, those qualities which make our whole life an acceptable and sweet-smelling sacrifice.

This testimony from God will be given to the heart which has faith, not only because faith is the very thing which is most God-glorifying and God-pleasing, but because it is the spiritual faculty which can recognise God's voice and witness. Faith is the death of the self-life, the silent waiting to allow God in his own hidden, mysterious way to speak to the soul and show himself to it. Faith is the opening of the heart in trust and love to receive what the Everlasting Love so longs to give – the full enjoyment of God's favour and approval. Such faith makes the walk with God what it is meant to be, the highest expression of the joy and the beauty of the Christian life, and the power by which death becomes a translation into the glory of the Presence in which we had already dwelt on earth.

By faith we walk with God. So let it be our one goal to believe and to let God be for us and do for us all that he can as God. Faith is the power by which we yield and give way to God, and allow him as God full freedom to do his utmost for us. If we live in Christ and walk in him, rooted and built up in him, we can and we do walk with God.

Chapter 15

By Faith We Please God

> *But without faith it is impossible to please [God]: for he that cometh to God must believe that he is, and that he is a rewarder of them that diligently seek him.* Hebrews 11:6

In the previous verse the writer has told us, 'By faith Enoch … had this testimony, that he pleased God.' He then pauses to enlarge upon this point and tells us that it was not only Enoch who pleased God in this way, but that it is the way for everyone. The law is universal: without faith it is impossible for anyone to please God. Each of God's servants has his particular calling and a work to do which is different from those given to the servants around him or the ones who will come after him. But there is one thing in which there is no change, whatever the time and circumstances: *Without faith it is impossible to please God.* The one thing which my God values every day and all the day in my every act of worship or of work is this: my faith in him. The one thing I need is this: that each moment, as my God looks upon me, he may see that I am 'full of faith'. What an amazing privilege that is – to be able to give pleasure to the eternal God! What an indescribable blessing, to know that I please him! Who could not want to learn the secret of such a life? We need to ponder the truth that it is by faith that we please God.

In studying what faith is, we must distinguish carefully between its nature and its effects. The greater part of chapter 11 of Hebrews is taken up with the description of its effects: faith obeys, faith waits, faith strengthens, faith fights and faith conquers. This is all the man-ward, world-ward aspect of faith, as the believer deals with the circumstances in which he finds himself. But if we want to know what faith really is in its true nature and essence, we must examine its God-ward aspect. Here lies its worth and its strength and its ability to please God and bless man.

Luther frequently used the expression, 'Let God be God.' He meant by this that we should give him the place which belongs to him as God, and let him do the work which, as God, he can and will do. This is the essence of faith: to let God be God, and so give him the glory. Faith fills the mind with the thought of God who, in the power of his infinite love, works out his purposes in the world, especially in his people, and personally in every believer who yields to him. Faith falls prostrate before this glorious Being and worships him as he orders everything according to his own will. Faith waits and cries and thirsts for God until he makes himself a divine reality to the soul and his Presence becomes nearer and clearer than anything else in existence. And so God reveals himself, and truly becomes God to the soul. He becomes all in all. By faith his glorious Presence rests on the soul.

In Hebrews 11:6 we have a description of God-pleasing faith, and in it the position which this faith must give to God is shown with remarkable clearness. Four times in the same verse God is placed in the foreground as the only object of faith: 'He that cometh to God must believe that he is, and that he is a rewarder of them that diligently seek him.'

'*He that cometh to God must believe.*' This is the place where faith is born. When a man is drawn by God to himself, when a man turns away from himself and all the world and wishes to meet and know the living God, when he truly wants to draw near to God, then he must believe. It is then that he will learn to believe. It in such believing that he will really come to God and know that he has found and met him.

'*... Must believe that he is.*' This is what our faith must first and foremost concentrate upon. This will also be its highest attainment: a sense, a consciousness and an impression – in some measure corresponding to the infinite reality – that God is. What an impression of its presence a magnificent mountain or a great ocean can give us if we just allow ourselves to take in its beauty and grandeur! And what an impression God could make upon us if we only yielded ourselves in adoring silence and let him breathe into us that sense of his Presence which is faith. If you want to be strong in faith, come to God, bow low before him and wait upon him until your soul is filled with the living assurance that he is. This is something infinitely better than believing a promise or believing for a special blessing. This is believing in God.

'*... That he is a rewarder.*' The verse does not say, '*... That there is a reward.*' No, our faith must say, '*He* is a rewarder.' It is directly from him, in personal contact with him, that the reward, the blessing, will be received. It is precisely because our faith is mostly more occupied with the reward than with the One who gives it that our efforts at believing are so futile. Oh, that men would learn to have faith in God! How easy faith in the promises would then become.

'... *A rewarder of them that diligently seek him.*' We hear a great deal about seeking salvation, but there is no such expression anywhere in Scripture. Instead it says, 'Seek the Lord', 'Seek my face', 'Your hearts shall live that seek God'. We should not so much seek blessing or power; rather, we should *seek God*. We need to *come to God*. We need to believe that *God is,* that he is the Rewarder of those who seek him. 'Acquaint thyself with God, and be at peace.'

Oh, my brother, do you wish to be a true believer, a strong believer? Then have the sort of faith which pleases God. Let the one desire of your soul be to have faith in him. Spend time in holy meditation and silent worship to seek him, to come to him, to learn first of all that he is, and only then that he is the Rewarder. Then you will begin to understand what faith is: the free gift of God, by which he opens up your being so that you may know him and receive all the wonderful reward of grace and strength which he gives to those who please him.

Chapter 16

Jesus, the Perfecter of Our Faith

> *Let us ... lay aside every weight, and the sin which doth so easily beset us, and let us run with patience the race that is set before us, looking unto Jesus, the author and perfecter of our faith.* Hebrews 12:1–2, RV

The practical and the contemplative aspects of the Christian life are often spoken of as being at odds with each other. But these words from Hebrews express them in their perfect unity. 'Let us lay aside every weight, and the sin which doth so easily beset us, and let us run': here we have expressed the active side of Christian life. We are encouraged to leave all hindrances behind, pursue sanctification and with all the energy we possess press on in the race. 'Looking unto Jesus': this is the inner life of meditation, waiting and worship. As we gaze upon the Lord and his glory, we will be changed into his likeness. So we are to run, and yet to look to Jesus at the same time.

Faith is the eye of the heart: as our spiritual vision beholds Jesus and remains fixed on him, then our feet will tread swiftly and surely in his footsteps. A deeper knowledge of Jesus, an eye never for a moment taken off him, is the secret of Christian progress. And why is this? Because Jesus is the Leader and Perfecter of our faith. Both of these terms have been used before in this Epistle. In chapter 2 Jesus was called the Leader of our salvation: 'It became him [God] … in bringing [or leading] many sons unto glory, to make the captain [or leader] of their salvation perfect through sufferings' (verse 10). In chapter 6 he was spoken of as the 'Forerunner', entering within the veil to open the way for us (verse 20). In chapter 10 he is depicted as the Leader of our faith. It was he who opened up for us a fresh and living way to God, the way of self-sacrifice in which he himself walked, and in which we are to walk too. He led in the way of faith. It was by faith that he lived his life. He is not only our Example in the life of faith, but our Leader and Forerunner in it too, and as such he helps us and draws us on. The Old Testament saints had given us examples of faith, but theirs was a faith which did not inherit all the promises. But Jesus is the Leader of *our faith*, a faith which passes through death into resurrection life, which enters the Holiest of all and ministers in the power of an endless life.

Looking unto such a Leader, we run the race with patience, because he is also the Perfecter of our faith. One of the great truths of this Epistle is that Christ's perfection is the secret of the Christian's perfection. He is the Perfecter of faith: he perfected it in his own person by acting it out to its fullest possibility when in death he entrusted his spirit to his Father's hands. By his faith he was himself perfected, and proved that perfect faith is the highest perfection, because it gives God room to be all. He, the Perfect One, who has perfected us in himself, is now the perfect object of our faith: he gives himself to us as the highest consummation of all that faith can ask or receive. He is the Perfecter of faith, because he lives and works in us in the power of his endless life and so perfects the faith which is in us. Our going on to perfection is now no hopeless task. It is possible for us to have the same perfect faith which he had, a faith which trusts God for everything. The faith which looks to Jesus, the Perfect One and the Perfecter, is the secret of Christian perfection. Let us run, looking unto Jesus, who in his life on earth was our Leader in faith, and who in his glory on the throne is now the Perfecter of our faith.

Jesus, 'for the joy that was set before him endured the cross, despising shame, and hath sat down at the right hand of the throne of God' (12:2, RV). We need to gaze lengthily upon him there, crowned with honour and glory, our High Priest at the right hand of the Majesty on high. We need to let every thought of him on the throne remind us of the path which brought him there, and which brings us there too. It is the path of faith, obedience, self-sacrifice and suffering – the path of the cross. There is no way into the Holiest of all but the one which Jesus has opened and dedicated. And we also need to let every thought of him in that path of faith and trial lift our hearts once again to the throne, where he reigns in divine authority as the Perfected One and the Perfecter, communicating to us the power of his death and victory – the power of his complete and eternal salvation.

Yes, let us run the race, looking unto Jesus, the Perfecter of our faith.

The Africa Evangelical Fellowship

The AEF is an international evangelical mission. For more information about their work, please contact them at their International office, 17 Westcote Road, Reading, Berks RG3 2DL.

The AEF has hundreds of opportunities for both long and short term service in evangelism, church planting, education, medical administration, youth work and other practical fields.

Other AEF offices are:-

Australia
PO Box 292
Castle Hill
New South Wales 2154

Canada
470 McNicoll Avenue
Willowdale
Ontario M2H 2E1

USA
PO Box 2896
Boone
North Carolina 28607

United Kingdom
30 Lingfield Road
Wimbledon
London SW19 4PU

Zimbabwe
99 Gaydon Road
Graystone Park
Borrowdale
Harare

South Africa
Rowland House
6 Montrose Avenue
Claremont 7700

New Zealand
PO Box 1390
Invercargill

Europe
5 Rue de Meautry
94500 Champigny-sur-Marne
France